HARNESSING UZBEKISTAN'S POTENTIAL OF URBANIZATION

NATIONAL URBAN ASSESSMENT

SEPTEMBER 2021

ADB

ASIAN DEVELOPMENT BANK

© 2021 Asian Development Bank
6 ADB Avenue, Mandaluyong City, 1550 Metro Manila, Philippines
Tel +63 2 8632 4444; Fax +63 2 8636 2444
www.adb.org

Some rights reserved. Published in 2021.

ISBN 978-92-9269-031-1 (print); 978-92-9269-032-8 (electronic); 978-92-9269-033-5 (ebook)
Publication Stock No. TCS210334-2
DOI: http://dx.doi.org/10.22617/TCS210334-2

The views expressed in this publication are those of the authors and do not necessarily reflect the views and policies of the Asian Development Bank (ADB) or its Board of Governors or the governments they represent.

ADB does not guarantee the accuracy of the data included in this publication and accepts no responsibility for any consequence of their use. The mention of specific companies or products of manufacturers does not imply that they are endorsed or recommended by ADB in preference to others of a similar nature that are not mentioned.

By making any designation of or reference to a particular territory or geographic area, or by using the term "country" in this document, ADB does not intend to make any judgments as to the legal or other status of any territory or area.

Please contact pubsmarketing@adb.org if you have questions or comments with respect to content, or if you wish to obtain copyright permission for your intended use that does not fall within these terms, or for permission to use the ADB logo.

Corrigenda to ADB publications may be found at http://www.adb.org/publications/corrigenda.

Note:
In this publication, "$" refers to United States dollars.

Cover design by Kookie Trivinio. Photos from ADB Photo Library.

Contents

Appendixes

Tables, Figures, and Maps

Tables

Figures

Maps

Acknowledgments

The Asian Development Bank (ADB) report team would like to express its sincere appreciation for the valuable time and inputs given by Uzbekistan's Ministry of Investments and Foreign Trade, Ministry of Economic Development and Poverty Reduction, and other government agencies in preparing this report. The team is also grateful for the valuable support provided by the Uzbekistan Resident Mission.

Team Leader: Ron Slangen, Principal Urban Development Specialist, ADB

Main Author: Anthony Gad Bigio, Urban Advisor (ADB consultant)

Research Support: Antonella Salmerón, Research Assistant (ADB consultant); Niels Van Dijk, Urban Specialist (ADB consultant); Mirodil Mirakhmedov, Institutional Specialist (ADB consultant)

Technical Reviewer: Hong Soo Lee, Senior Urban Development Specialist (Smart Cities), ADB

Abbreviations

ADB	Asian Development Bank
CAGR	compounded annual growth rate
CAREC	Central Asia Regional Economic Cooperation
CIS	Commonwealth of Independent States
COVID-19	coronavirus disease
DHC	district heating companies
FDI	foreign direct investment
GDP	gross domestic product
GFDRR	Global Facility for Disaster Reduction and Recovery
GIS	geographic information system
IFI	international financial institution
LLC	Limited Liability Company
MHCS	Ministry of Housing and Communal Services
MIFT	Ministry of Investment and Foreign Trade
Mtoe	million tonnes of oil equivalent
NRW	non-revenue water
PPP	public–private partnership
PRC	People's Republic of China
SCEEP	State Committee on Ecology and Environmental Protection
SNG	subnational government
SOE	state-owned enterprise
SWM	solid waste management
WHO	World Health Organization
WSS	water supply and sanitation

Executive Summary

Five years after Uzbekistan opened its economy to regional and global trade and investments, the government has taken steps to leverage from the opportunities offered by urbanization. Harnessing values and assets that have been so far constrained, such as rural labor and urban land, in favor of sustainable urban development, will help diversify the national economy and contribute to stronger and more equitable future growth. This National Urban Assessment reveals key population, economic, and policy trends linked to urbanization. It also identifies the present hurdles and ways for the country to overcome them. The assessment is based on extensive consultations with various stakeholders, including government and development partners. Field visits, data collection, analysis, and literature review were also conducted.

On 11 March 2020, the World Health Organization (WHO) declared the coronavirus disease (COVID-19) as a global pandemic. COVID-19 has impacted the day-to-day lives of Uzbekistan citizens, disrupting urban life and causing physical, social, and economic distress, particularly to poor and vulnerable people in cities. This report highlights integrated and strategic development as an approach to effectively build back better and to strengthen resilience and long-term recovery. It is consistent with ADB's *Livable Cities: Post-COVID-19 New Normal Guidance Note*. Harnessing urbanization can attract countercyclical investments in urban development, including construction of urban infrastructure and housing, thereby creating additional value, jobs, and welfare opportunities at a time of global economic downturn and uncertainty due to the COVID-19 pandemic.

Part I: State of the Urban Sector

Since Uzbekistan's independence, urbanization in the country has lagged behind, leading to significant regional imbalances. Currently at just above 50%, the rate of urbanization has been inflated by the past administrative reclassification of rural settlements. National mobility constraints caused a significant level of out-migration, and low urban housing affordability further stifled rural to urban movement. More than half of the urban population is concentrated in 7.5% of the national territory, in the easternmost regions. Tashkent dominates the urban hierarchy and hosts much stronger urban economic activities and quality of urban infrastructure than all other cities. The national economy is still dominated by state-owned enterprises, with the private sector in its infancy. The informal economy, coupled with remittances, still provides more than half of household earnings.

Urban governance is highly centralized and municipalities have uncertain mandates and resources. Governance in Uzbekistan is partially deconcentrated, with appointed regional governors and mayors. Line ministries and related agencies are responsible for the design and implementation of urban investment programs and for the centralized management of urban services. With the exception of the capital city, municipalities are subject to the jurisdiction of regional governors in the allocation of mandates and resources. Subnational governments are responsible for 70% of public expenditure, only a fraction of which is devoted to urban systems and quality of life, and for the collection of 30% of fiscal revenues. Budget transfers are neither formula-based nor responsive to performance which discourages efficient and transparent public financial management.

Housing and urban infrastructure and services have declined and do not provide for sufficient livability. Uzbekistan's housing stock is old and ill-maintained. Housing units, including traditional individual low-rise houses and Soviet Union-period apartment blocks, were privatized after independence and are properly recorded in the cadastral system. Yearly supply of new housing is well below the demand levels and urban housing affordability is very low. Urban planning is antiquated and does not provide for integrated frameworks or for strategic, local economic development. Water supply, sanitation, solid waste management, district heating, and energy and gas systems have suffered from a lack of capital investment and systematic maintenance, and from non-market pricing of services. Urban road networks are incomplete and public spaces underequipped. Urban transit systems have been mostly abandoned in favor of individual motorization. Overall, urban livability is low across Uzbekistan's cities.

Environmental degradation, urban natural hazards, and climate change risks are increasing. Water scarcity is significant and expected to increase by 45% by 2030—affecting urban supply if unattended—due to increased transboundary usage and climate change. The quality of urban environment and public health is affected by the unsanitary disposal of solid waste and wastewater, including municipal and industrial effluent causing severe water pollution. Air pollution is also considerable, resulting from industrial emissions, suspended dusts, toxic chemicals, and particulates from indoor stoves. Uzbek cities are exposed to a high level of seismic and flooding risks due to glacial lake outburst, deforestation, and landslides. Climate change is altering precipitations and ambient temperatures, making heat waves more frequent and intense.

Part II: Government Policies and Programs

Policy orientations support urbanization and urban development, however, institutional capacity is low. In 2017, the new government identified accelerating urbanization as an important part of its reform agenda, targeting 60% by 2030, together with a more balanced regional development pattern and free territorial mobility. The 2019 Presidential Decree on Urbanization laid the foundation for a new generation of urban policies. To pursue their implementation, the Agency for Urbanization was subsequently created under the Ministry of Economic Development and Poverty Reduction. A year later, the ministry was replaced by the Department for the Implementation of Urbanization Policies. Unclear coordination mechanism continues to exist among line ministries. Institutional capacity for moving forward the process of urbanization is currently low.

Reforms and investments are progressing in many critical areas. Some advances have been made in fiscal decentralization in favor of municipalities. A law and an agency for public–private partnerships were established. Housing finance reform is underway, which could boost access to credit by households, with a greater involvement of the private sector. A neighborhood upgrading program was established and initially financed. Progress has been made in the institutional reforms of the agencies managing water supply and sanitation, solid waste, and energy generation and distribution; and investments have supported such reforms. The government also works to improve district heating, gas distribution, and pollution management. However, land privatization has just started and implementation capacity to execute urban sector reforms is a challenge. Most recently, a new Cadaster Agency was established under the State Tax Committee.

Multilateral institutions, including the Asian Development Bank, support Uzbekistan's urban development. A number of international financial institutions (IFIs), in addition to the Asian Development Bank (ADB), are working with the government in the urban sector, under loans and grants of nearly $3.0 billion to date. Of its

$7.5 billion of total lending to the country, ADB has invested $950 million in urban infrastructure and is preparing its first integrated urban development project for approval in 2022. The World Bank, the second-largest provider of international finance, is also present in the urban sector and supporting integrated approaches, institutional capacity building, and analytical work. Following its Strategy 2030 Operational Plan for Priority 4: Making Cities More Livable, ADB will implement urban sustainability programs and projects that will support Uzbek cities to become competitive, green and resilient, equitable, and inclusive.

Part III: Challenges in Sustainable Urbanization to 2030

Directing future urbanization. If the current trends are simply maintained, it is unlikely for the government to achieve its goal of a 60% rate of urbanization by 2030. Uzbekistan's urban population has slightly declined from 51.5% in 2010 to 50.5% in 2019. This trend reflects a mix of factors, including domestic migration restrictions (named *propiska*), higher cost of living in urban areas, and a mismatch of skills sets with urban employment opportunities. While the government's lifting of the *propiska* system is likely to stimulate increases in rural-to-urban migration, achieving the government's target of 60% urbanization by 2030 is a challenge. Various dynamics, whether policy driven or not, could reverse such trends in the coming decade. Proactive urbanization through strategic, well-coordinated, evidence-based, and integrated planning and investments particularly in secondary cities, combined with responsive urban governance, would make these areas more attractive for businesses and residents. If left uncoordinated, however, future urbanization will further exacerbate regional imbalances. The government should seek alternative ways to reinforce the role of secondary cities and regional hubs, such as Samarkand, Bukhara and Karshi, and of smaller ones, such as Urgench and Nukus in the northwest, as well as Djizzak and Gulistan located between Tashkent and Samarkand. This would move Uzbekistan toward a polycentric development and support regional development, enhancing opportunities for growth and welfare.

Supporting municipal development. Accelerating decentralization is an area of reform that plays an important role in supporting equitable urbanization, as cities become the focus of economic development and as more complex entities require more advanced management systems. Decentralization would require reviewing and clarifying the assignments of functions across government levels; improving the transparency and predictability of budget transfers through a rule-based system (such as in Indonesia); and providing greater revenue autonomy to subnational governments. Assigning municipalities a greater role in urban development will require improving their technical, organizational, and financial capacities.

Reforming urban planning. A new generation of urban master plans would translate a national urbanization strategy into both medium- and long-term growth strategies for Uzbekistan's capital and for its secondary cities. These plans aim to enhance livability by facilitating urban competitiveness; equitable urban redevelopment; better access to urban services; and improvements in public health, environmental quality, and resilience to natural hazards and climate change risks. They would promote bottom-up planning processes, capitalize on comparative advantages (both economic and location), and allow for integrated urban development, bringing together the multiple components required for urban livability, instead of the traditional top-down planning approach that separates various urban systems and investments.

Enabling territorial mobility. A legacy of the Soviet Union era, residency permits are required nationwide, which significantly constrain urbanization. Violators of the procedure are mostly the vulnerable, low-income migrants from rural areas, estimated at 320,000 to more than 1 million in Tashkent; secondary cities are also affected. In April 2020, the residency permit system was relaxed for Tashkent and its region, granting official residence in return for the purchase of a housing unit. Housing, however, is largely unaffordable to low-income unregistered migrants. One of the goals of Urbanization Decree 2019 is "free movement of people from rural to urban areas," and this should be fully implemented.

Increasing urban housing and infrastructure supply. Assuming territorial mobility will be achieved, a major increase in affordable urban housing supply is needed, considering the additional internal migration levels and the accumulated supply backlog. Scaling up urbanization and urban development in the country also requires a significant increase in the provision of urban infrastructure and services that essentially complement the supply of housing. This requires capable sector institutions, major financial investments, robust regulatory frameworks, and financial set ups, including tariffs allowing for full cost recovery. As per the Presidential Decree 6074 (September 2020), tariffs are now required for the water and sanitation sector to further develop drinking water supply and sewerage system. Opportunities for private sector participation would help meet the current gaps.

Addressing environmental degradation. For Uzbekistan's urbanization to become sustainable, addressing the environmental and climate change constraints would avoid a pattern of urban dependency on high consumption of water and energy and increasing carbon emissions. Anticipatory urban planning and urban resiliency should be a priority. Stronger policy, regulatory, and enforcement mechanisms are required to achieve higher environmental standards. Investment programs could expand the use of renewable energy systems in urban areas to supplement the centralized provision of urban services, such as energy and district heating.

Part IV: Making Uzbek Cities More Livable

Uzbek cities can become more competitive, green and resilient, equitable, and inclusive. Trade facilitation policies, border improvements, and local infrastructure upgrades in the urban centers along transport corridors would generate agglomeration benefits and support the development of secondary cities. Higher urban density would be pursued via strategic urban master plans that reflect an integrated vision of urban growth to benefit residents, firms, and other economic actors. The master plans also aim to achieve urban efficiency. Privatizing urban land would equitably create and distribute wealth among households, as well as unlock economic opportunities. Other options include long-term leasehold schemes, such as those in Singapore, which could be further explored. Area redevelopment plans would be designed with the communities and public interests in mind, in addition to market potential.

There are multiple opportunities for further ADB engagement in the urban sector to 2030. Through the the Integrated Urban Development Project in Uzbekistan, ADB will deepen the dialogue with the government to identify areas for further collaboration. Technical assistance and lending could be developed to (i) enhance city and regional competitiveness, (ii) support decentralization and financial sustainability, (iii) strengthen urban governance, (iv) meet urban infrastructure needs, and (v) improve urban livability.

I.   State of the Urban Sector

Population and Urbanization

Demographics

Uzbekistan had a population of 33,724,900 as of 1 October 2019.[1] This number is estimated against a baseline of 20,398,348 in 1990, as the last full census was conducted in 1989. Since then, the Uzbekistan State Commission of Statistics (USCS) has been carrying out only periodic sample surveys of 10% of the population and applying a related national annual demographic growth rate, which has tapered off from 2.46% in 1990 to 1.48% in 2020.[2] The next general census is scheduled in 2022. While the Institute of Makhalla provides useful demographic data for the Government of Uzbekistan, a key challenge for the country is the consolidation and processing of data to support updated analysis of demographic and urbanization trends.

Uzbekistan's life expectancy at birth is 73.9 years (2018). Its pyramid of age shows a significant "youth bulge" of ages 18 to 35, causing pressures on the internal labor market and migration mainly to Kazakhstan, the Republic of Korea, the Russian Federation, Turkey, the United Arab Emirates, and European countries. Immigrants from neighboring countries represent 3.9% of the total population (2015), while the net migration rate is negative at -1.6/1,000 inhabitants (2015–2020).[3] About 45% of the national population and 56% of the urban population are concentrated in the Tashkent region and capital city and in the three regions of the Fergana Valley, the easternmost part of the country. These four regions, however, jointly account for just 7.5% of the national territory.

Status and Key Urbanization Trends

As of 2019, the urban population of Uzbekistan was 16,807,000 (50.5% of the country's total population). This figure has declined slightly compared to 51.5% in 2010. The 2009 reclassification of various rural settlements as "urban" contributed to an increase of urbanization, which was only 37.4% in 2000. Low urbanization is symptomatic of various economic and policy constraints in the country. Uzbekistan has a total of 119 cities of various population sizes and 1,071 urban settlements, which are statistically defined as settlements located in the rural areas but wherein employment is predominantly non-agricultural. The ranking of urban centers shows the prevalence of small towns (80) and of medium-sized cities (21), with 10 big cities and 7 large ones (Table 1). Tashkent as the "primate city" is overwhelmingly larger.[4]

---

[1]   The State Committee of Republic of Uzbekistan on Statistics. 2020. Demographic Indicators (accessed 1 May 2020).
[2]   World Population Review. 2020. Uzbekistan Population 2020 (accessed 1 May 2020).
[3]   International Organization for Migration. 2016. Uzbekistan (accessed 1 May 2020).
[4]   A city is defined as "primate" if it is disproportionally larger in the national urban hierarchy. M. Jefferson. 1939. The Law of the Primate City. *Geographical Review*. 29 (2).

Table 1: Ranking of Urban Centers by Population Size

Types of Urban Centers	Ranking by Population Size	Number
Urban settlements	undefined	1,071
Small towns	< 50,000	80
Medium-sized cities	50,001–100,000	21
Big cities	100,000–250,000	10
Large cities	250,000–1,000,000	7
Capital city	2,500,000	1
Total number of urban centers		**1,190**

Source: Uzbekistan State Commission on Statistics. 2020.

The trajectory of urbanization by region for 2000 and 2019, with linear growth projections to 2030 (based on growth rates between 2010 and 2019) is presented in Appendix 1, together with illustrative maps. Besides the capital city of Tashkent, the seven largest cities are Andijan, Fergana, and Namangan in the Fergana Valley; Bukhara, Karshi, and Samarkand in the south; and Nukus in the northwest. Of these, only three (Andijan, Namangan, and Samarkand) have a population of about 500,000; the other four have a population of about 300,000 each. Unofficial estimates put Tashkent's population at about 4 million on account of non-registered migrants. This eightfold gap between the capital and the three largest secondary cities, coupled with the concentration of more than half of the population in the eastern regions, should be considered when planning toward a more balanced territorial development of the country in the next decade.

The historically low rate of urbanization is correlated with past restrictions on internal mobility imposed through the government's control of residency permits (*propiska*), which has limited internal migration. Urbanization is also hampered by the limited supply of affordable housing in the main urban centers, and higher cost of living in

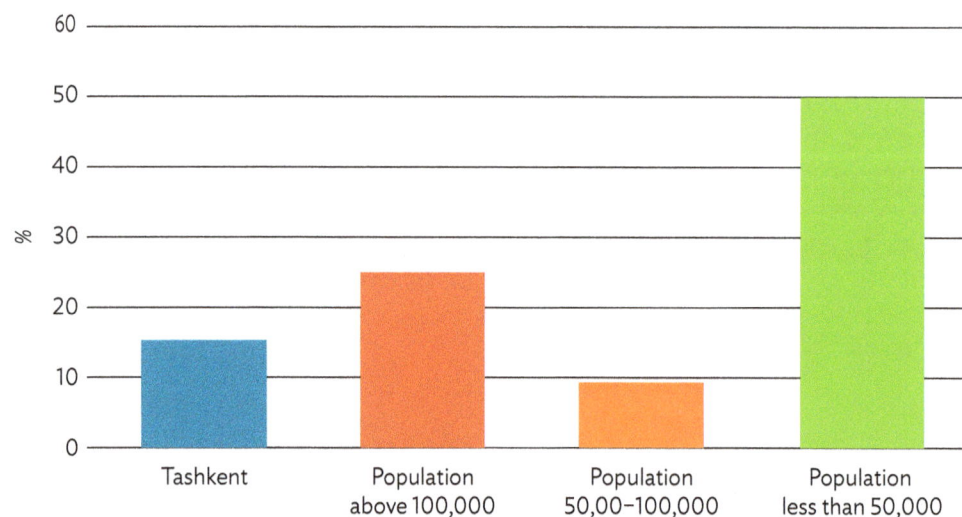

Figure 1: Uzbekistan's Distribution of Urban Population by City Size

Source: World Bank. 2017.

cities.[5] According to the World Bank, 50% of the urban population resides in towns of under 50,000 inhabitants, which have also been growing faster than the other urban centers.[6] As urban economic opportunities are concentrated in the larger centers, these hurdles particularly constrain internal migration to these areas.

Regional Disparities

Uzbekistan's territory is subdivided administratively into 12 regions, the Republic of Karakalpakstan (an autonomous entity with its own governance system), and the capital city of Tashkent, which has a special status equivalent to a region. The 2019 rates of urbanization of the different jurisdictions vary considerably, from a minimum of 33.2% for the Khorezm region to 72.8% for the Tashkent region, including the data for the capital.

Such disparities among Uzbekistan's regions are related to several variables, which include geographic locations, very different natural and climatic environments, economic roles, and levels of connectivity provided by transport and trade routes. The main roads and railways provide effective functional links among the cities of the southern part of the country, while the northwestern region of Khorezm and the Republic of Karakalpakstan are relatively isolated and count on international rail corridors for trade as well as for passenger trips and on passenger air links to the capital city itself.

In 2009, the Center for Economic Research (CER) conducted a comparative evaluation of the aggregate Regional Development Index of Uzbekistan, by comparing the quality of life, economic competitiveness, and infrastructure development indicator scores of each region. It reveals that the city of Tashkent's Regional Development Index score of 0.9 is two to three times higher than those of the other regions.[7]

Functional Roles of Capital, Secondary, and Satellite Cities

With a history of significant public sector investments in its infrastructure, productive base, and urban services provision since Russian then Soviet Union times, Tashkent confirms its role as the lead city, scoring highest on all indicators. Its attractiveness spills over the other cities that form the big regional Tashkent agglomeration: Almalyk, Angren, Akhangaran, Yangiyul, and Chirchik.

Of the seven main secondary cities, Andijan, Namangan, and Fergana act as the urban hubs of the Fergana Valley, which combines intensive agricultural activities with important industrial enterprises in the textile, automotive, and logistics sectors. Given the isolated nature of the valley and its transportation hurdles, these cities count on their proximity to the Tashkent region and the capital city for access to markets. Samarkand and Bukhara, in addition to having central economic functions in regions of agricultural prevalence, also attract tourists on account of their history and heritage.

Agriculture is the dominant sector of the Kashkadarya region, of which Karshi is the main urban center, and its economy reflects the related trading activities. As the capital of Karakalpakstan, Nukus' key function is administrative. The economic activities of the city are constrained by the low quality of life, low levels of competitiveness, limited job offers and business opportunities, and low infrastructure development scores of the region (footnote 7). The impacts of transport corridors, trade, and logistics on cities is further reviewed in section 3.

---

[5]   W. Seitz. 2020. Free Movement and Affordable Housing—Public Preferences for Reform in Uzbekistan. *Policy Research Working Paper* 9107. Washington, DC: World Bank. January.

[6]   World Bank. Uzbekistan Urban Policy Note. Unpublished.

[7]   Center for Economic Research. 2009. Urbanization and Industrialization in Uzbekistan: Challenges, Problems and Prospects. *Policy Brief* 2009/01. Tashkent.

A number of smaller towns gravitate around Uzbekistan's large, big, and medium-sized cities, as functional production and consumption links extend well beyond the urban jurisdictional boundaries. Some of these "satellite cities" may transform into medium-sized or large cities, and urban boundaries extended, but at the cost of perpetuating the current, inefficient, low-density urban sprawl model. Region-scale analyses such as those conducted for Djizzak and Syrdarya regions by ADB,[8] and for the Khorezm region by the European Bank for Reconstruction and Development (EBRD), are valuable demonstration exercises for identifying ways to address optimal regional territorial strategies, and should be applied throughout the country as a routine instrumental planning exercise carried out by the government.

Economy and Employment

Economic Impacts of COVID-19

In 2020, following the COVID-19 pandemic, Uzbekistan's gross domestic product (GDP) decreased from 5.8% to 1.6% with significant declines in tourism, trade, construction, and remittances. Unemployment expanded from 9.0% to 11%.[9] COVID-19 and associated lockdowns reduced fiscal revenues from 28.2% of GDP in 2019 to 27.9% in 2020. Sharp declines in urban revenues, including from water supply and sanitation (WSS) utilities, put added pressure on the delivery of basic urban services. In response to the COVID-19 pandemic, the government aims to (i) preserve income and livelihoods, especially for the poor and vulnerable; (ii) prevent long-term damage to the economy; and (iii) safeguard economic transition and reform.

Main Sectors of the Formal Economy

Uzbekistan is in the midst of transitioning from a command–and–control to a market-based economy. The transition started in 1991 after Uzbekistan gained independence. Since 2017, however, the country has taken a rapid and tangible path with the liberalization of foreign exchange, tax reform, and a major upgrade in economic statistics. It is a low–middle income country. Its GDP per capita went from $2,576 in 2016 to $1,810 in 2017, to $1,550 (estimated) in 2018 to $1,832 (projected) in 2019.[10] Such fluctuations are evidence of the national economy's dependence on the prices of Uzbekistan's main export commodities, such as gold, copper and other minerals, oil and gas, and cotton. In 2019, industry accounted for 36.4% of GDP, agriculture 28%, and services 35.6%.[11] As a result of its reform agenda leading to GDP growth above 5%, Uzbekistan was labeled "country of the year" in 2019.[12]

Traditionally, the economy has mostly relied on state-owned enterprises (SOEs) across all sectors in creating wealth and employment and in providing welfare. Being the key providers of formal employment, SOEs have benefited from preferential access to natural resources, such as land, water, energy and minerals, as well as to financial credit. Some large SOEs had to take care of housing, health care, and other social services for their employees, having established and managed such costly non-core activities at the request of the government or regional authorities. Consequently, this forced the majority of SOEs to file for bankruptcy due to the excessive expenses directed away from their core services and activities. The opening of the economy in 2017 called into question the dominant role of approximately 8,000 active SOEs.

---

[8]   ADB. 2020. *Technical Assistance to the Republic of Uzbekistan for Preparing Urban Development and Improvement Projects: Strategic Urban and Regional Development Planning for Syrdarya and Djizzak Regions.* Manila.

[9]   ADB. 2021. *Asian Development Outlook.* Manila.

[10] International Monetary Fund. 2019. Article IV Consultation Staff Report. Washington, DC. 9 May.

[11] The State Committee of Republic of Uzbekistan on Statistics. 2020. Volume of Gross Domestic Product of the Republic of Uzbekistan by Types of Economic Activities. Tashkent.

[12] *The Economist.* 2019. Country of the Year: Which Nation Improved the Most in 2019? London. 21 December.

Figure 2: Age Dependency Ratio, Uzbekistan, 1990–2018

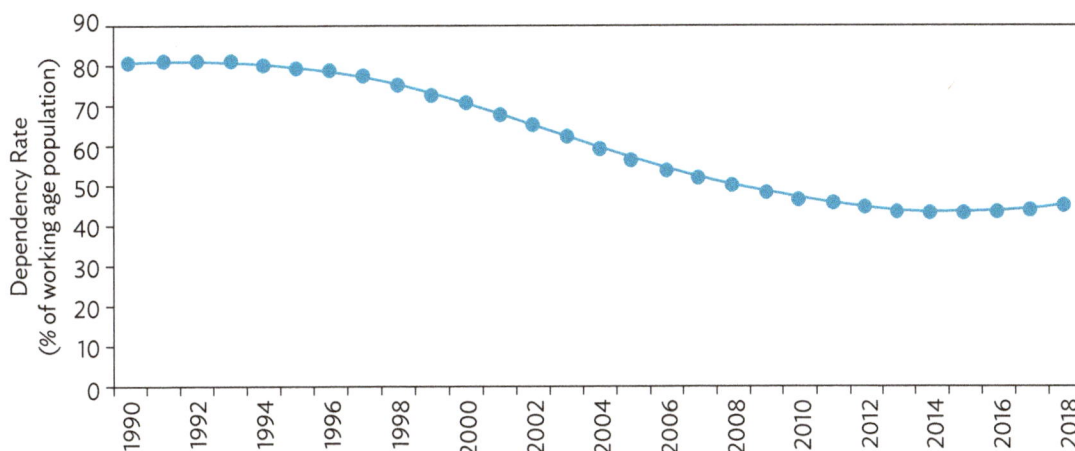

Source: World Bank. World Development Indicator. http://databank.worldbank.org/ (accessed 11 November 2019).

In particular, job creation has been scarce and insufficient in view of the youth bulge, causing rising unemployment, out-migration, and dissatisfaction, especially among the youth. An estimated 500,000 individuals will enter the labor force every year until 2030. The age dependency ratio (Figure 2) has been falling continuously since 2000 and is expected to remain unusually low in the coming decades. However, the formal private sector is nascent and currently employs only 11% of the working age population. Of the 3,050 large private firms present in 2013, only 2,300 were left in 2016, while small firms had grown from 190,000 in 2013 to 210,000 in 2016. Production is highly energy- and water-intensive, while resources are scarce.[13] Opportunities for the growth of private sector activities are significant, including manufacturing of goods for export (e.g., textiles, fertilizers, cars, home appliances, food).[14] The country is implementing ambitious market-oriented economic reforms. However, such reforms would require further liberalizing access to resources, investments, and credit and creating an enabling environment.

Informal Economic Activities

Since Soviet Union times, Uzbekistan has had an informal economy consisting of subsistence agriculture and construction activities and uncontrolled commerce of goods and services running in parallel with its formal, centralized economy. This dualism has persisted after independence, given the collapse of a number of publicly controlled industrial activities due to the break-up of the former Soviet Union production system and of the economic linkages between its member republics. Consequently, formal jobs were lost as well as access to the social services provided by the industrial conglomerates.

---

[13] International Finance Corporation. 2019. Country Private Sector Diagnostics: Creating Markets in Uzbekistan. World Bank Group Presentation to the Government of Uzbekistan. Tashkent. 18 February.
[14] World Bank. 2019. Uzbekistan Country Economic Update: Toward a New Economy. Washington, DC.

A recent survey conducted in 2018 by the Ministry of Employment in 62 cities and districts, covering 3,100 households and 16,425 citizens, reveals that 58.9% of national employment is in the informal sector.[15] In the current transition phase, as in other Commonwealth of Independent States (CIS) countries, the informal economy of Uzbekistan also represents a consistent share of GDP formation, estimated at 29% to 33% for 2015–2016 by the International Statistical Commission of the CIS.[16]

The coexistence of the formal and the informal economy marks the daily lives of Uzbek citizens, who often straddle both to make ends meet. This dualism also generates opportunities for corruption, as informal activities may be "tolerated" by officials in return for bribes.[17] The complex relationship between the two economies has been examined by sociologists and anthropologists. They analyze the post-Soviet Union citizens' experience of living in nations that are dismantling their previous productive and welfare infrastructure, and are confronted with the parallel emergence of powerful private sector entrepreneurs, some of whom double up as public officials.[18]

Socioeconomic Profile of the Population

Reliable information on the socioeconomic profile of the population is scarce, and more granular data covering the urban segment of the population is not available. The latest 2019 Household Survey on the Comprehensive Income of the Population (footnote 15) shows an average per capita yearly income of $479, with a higher average of $927 for Tashkent city and the lowest numbers for Karakalpakstan ($343), Namangan ($343), and Fergana ($365) regions. The survey reports an average income increase of 5.2% over 2018, when adjusted for inflation.

The composition of the average per capita income confirms the importance of the informal economy, at over 40%, and of remittances, at over 14%, as sources of income (Table 2). Regional variations in the income from formal sector jobs are not reported in this survey.

Unemployment in 2018 was at 9.3% and youth unemployment was particularly high at 17.4%, according to official figures. These also put out-migration of labor at 2 million for the year. However, unofficial figures point rather to 4 million, out of a total workforce estimated at 11.6 million.[19]

Table 2: Composition of the Average per Capita Income, 2019

Source of Per Capita Average Income	Percentage
Formal employment	28.5
Self-employment	40.9
Social transfers (pensions, benefits, scholarships)	10.5
Other transfers (remittances)	14.3
Property income (real estate and financial, of which 66% found in Tashkent city)	3.7
Subsistence activities (own production of services for own consumption)	2.1

Source: Uzbekistan State Commission on Statistics.

[15]   The State Committee of Republic of Uzbekistan on Statistics. 2019. *Sample Household Survey.*

[16]   T. K. Bekzhanova and A. B. Temirova. 2019. Non-Observed Economy as a Part of the Developing Economy. *Reports of the National Academy of Sciences of the Republic of Kazakhstan.* 2 (324). pp. 215–222. Tashkent.

[17]   Uzbekistan ranks 153 out of 180 countries in Transparency International's 2019 Corruption Perception Index.

[18]   J. Rasanayagam. 2011. Informal Economy, Informal State: The Case of Uzbekistan. *International Journal of Sociology and Social Policy.* 31 (11/12). pp. 681–696. Aberdeen.

[19]   ADB. 2019. *Country Partnership Strategy: Uzbekistan, 2019–2023 Supporting Economic Transformation.* Manila.

Regional Linkages

Uzbekistan's Trade Routes

Uzbekistan, one of only two double-landlocked countries in the world, has long been a land of trade routes linking Asia to Europe, the Silk Roads.[20] International commerce had established some of Uzbekistan's cities, most notably Samarkand and Bukhara, as well as the cities of the Fergana Valley, as trading posts of global reputation. Soviet Union colonization since the mid-19th century had changed the economic geography of the region and redirected trade from south to north, from the previous east–west axis. Soviet Union invested in railway construction and urban development with the establishment and build-up of Tashkent as the capital of Central Asia.

Uzbekistan's exports in 2017 were valued at $8.3 billion (Table 3). Top export destinations were (i) Switzerland ($3.68 billion) absorbing all of Uzbekistan's precious metals; (ii) the People's Republic of China (PRC) ($1.40 billion) purchasing mineral products, textiles, chemicals, and metals; (iii) the Russian Federation ($1.01 billion) purchasing textiles, plastics and rubber, and vegetable products; (iv) Turkey ($815 million) purchasing metals, textiles, plastics, and rubber; and (v) Kazakhstan ($714 million) purchasing vegetable products, mineral products, plastics and rubber, and textiles. Switzerland excluded, the same four key trading partners—the PRC, the Russian Federation, Kazakhstan, and Turkey—are the source of about two-thirds of all Uzbekistan's imports.[21]

Table 3: Composition of Uzbekistan's Exports, 2017

Export products	($ billion)	Percentage
Precious metals (gold)	3.74	45.0
Textiles	1.27	15.0
Metals	0.80	9.6
Mineral products (petroleum and gas)	0.74	8.9
Vegetable products	0.63	7.5
Plastic and rubber	0.44	5.3
Chemicals	0.35	4.3
Other	0.33	4.4
Total	**8.30**	**100.0**

Source: Observatory of Economic Complexity, MIT Media Lab.

Uzbekistan's present-day transport corridors, including both railways and trunk roads, connect the country: (i) north to Kazakhstan via the urban nodes of Tashkent and Nukus, (ii) southwest to Turkmenistan via the urban node of Bukhara, (iii) south to Afghanistan via the cities of Karshi and Termez, (iv) south again to Tajikistan via Samarkand and the cities of the Fergana Valley, and (v) east to the Kyrgyz Republic and the PRC via the Fergana Valley. Such transport corridors provide connectivity of varying quality for freight and passenger services alike. Trade and logistics are directly affected by the state of the transport system. Appendix 2 shows the map of transport corridors and related urban nodes.

---

[20]   The other one being Liechtenstein.
[21]   Observatory of Economic Complexity. 2020. Uzbekistan. Tashkent (accessed 1 May 2020).

CAREC, Belt and Road Initiative Corridors, and Uzbek cities

The Central Asia Regional Economic Cooperation (CAREC) Program, established by ADB in 1997, is a partnership of 11 countries and development partners working together to promote development through cooperation, leading to accelerated economic growth and poverty reduction.[22] The program is a proactive facilitator of practical, results-based regional projects, and policy initiatives critical to sustainable economic growth and shared prosperity in the region. Since its inception in 2001 and as of September 2019, CAREC has mobilized more than $34.5 billion investments that have helped establish multimodal transportation networks, increased energy trade and security, facilitated free movement of people and freight, and laid the groundwork for economic corridor development.[23]

Uzbekistan is benefiting from CAREC connectivity investments that aim to establish stronger linkages from the PRC to Europe and from Kazakhstan to Pakistan. Under CAREC, regional integration in Central Asia has been growing rapidly. Bilateral trade between Kazakhstan and Uzbekistan increased by 31.2% in 2017 alone, with oil deliveries from Kazakhstan expected to increase tenfold to 2 million tons a year by 2019. The turnover of trade between Uzbekistan and Tajikistan increased by 20 times between 2014 and 2018. In 2017, Uzbekistan and Turkmenistan opened a new railway border bridge, west of Bukhara. Relations between Uzbekistan and Tajikistan have also been improving.[24]

CAREC is currently implementing six main transport corridors (Appendix 2). Corridors 2, 3, and 6 directly affect Uzbekistan. A part of CAREC's work on corridor 2, the Karakalpakstan Road Project, will connect the Kungrad district to Kazakhstan. The A380 highway that connects Karakalpakstan with the Khorezm and Bukhara regions will be improved, facilitating the transportation of fuel, agricultural commodities, and industrial consumer goods. Corridor 3 has already connected Tashkent with Shymkent, a major industrial city in Kazakhstan, with a four-lane road. Corridor 6 includes the Ayni–Uzbekistan Border Road Improvement Project that will upgrade a part of the historical Silk Road, which was originally paved during the Soviet Union era. This project will benefit the city of Samarkand by improving the links to Tajikistan via the Panjakent border.

The CAREC program includes the electrification of the Bukhara–Khiva railway line; the Uzbekistan railway efficiency improvement project; the electrification of the Pap–Namangan–Andijan railway in the Fergana Valley; the construction of the electrified Angren–Pap railway, with the electrification of the Pap–Kokand–Andijan section, also in the Fergana Valley; and the railway electrification of the Kashi–Bukhara line with the organization of high-speed passenger trains. Uzbek Railways has been recently established, and now operates the Afrosiyob high-speed passenger railway line linking Tashkent and Samarkand.

The Belt and Road Initiative will also provide additional rail investments that will impact Uzbekistan's connectivity: (i) the new rail line connecting Kashgar (PRC) to Tashkent via Andijan, where a new transport hub will likely open; (ii) the Samarkand–Mashhad rail upgrade from Uzbekistan to Iran; and (iii) three more rail gateways to be added to the existing ones along the corridors toward the Russian Federation (Navoyi, Urgench, and Tashkent). Corridors toward Iran and South Asia through Turkmenistan and Afghanistan would also develop the southern transport hubs of Samarkand and Bukhara.[25]

---

[22] Afghanistan, Azerbaijan, Georgia, Kazakhstan, Kyrgyz Republic, Mongolia, Pakistan, People's Republic of China, Tajikistan, Turkmenistan, and Uzbekistan.

[23] CAREC Institute. CAREC Program.

[24] P. Frankopan. 2018. *The New Silk Roads: The Present and Future of the World.* London.

[25] S. Lall and M. Lebrand. 2019. Who Wins, Who Loses? Understanding the Spatially Differentiated Effects of the Belt and Road Initiative. *Policy Research Working Paper* 8806. Washington, DC: World Bank.

Foreign Direct Investment

Foreign direct investment (FDI) is clearly incentivized by upgrading transport and trade facilitation in Uzbekistan. While still only 1.2% of total GDP, FDI increased fourfold to $400 million in 2018.[26] Almost 50% of Uzbekistan's FDI benefits the coal, oil, and natural gas industries. The Russian Federation remains the most important investor in Uzbekistan, contributing 55% of FDI, followed by the PRC at 15%.[27]

The World Bank is assisting the Government of Uzbekistan in transitioning Tashkent, Bukhara, Fergana, and Urgench airports to external management by a reputable operator expected to invest and manage all airport facilities. The government and the Ministry of Transport are considering proposals and terms for the operation of the Samarkand airport. A number of private foreign companies, including from Japan and the Russian Federation, have expressed interest. The Tashkent Metro will receive financing from the Vnesheconombank State Development Corporation to supply five metro trains and related materials and technical facilities and services. The Vnesheconombank financed the modernization of two power units of the Syrdarya Thermal Power Plant, the largest plant in Uzbekistan, and is currently working on four more power units. Other countries such as Japan and the Republic of Korea have shown interest in investing in Uzbekistan. Kawasaki Heavy Industries from Japan announced a $940 million investment on a high-efficiency gas turbine cogeneration system in the city of Fergana.

The government established 21 free economic zones to attract further FDI and incentivize related industrial activities, and in relation to increasing transboundary trade opportunities with Tajikistan and Kazakhstan. Free economic zones enjoy special fiscal exemptions and other incentives to investors.[28] Some well-established industrial cities in the Tashkent region and three other regions benefit from a special status ("Republican subordination"), wherein they are under the direct administration of the central authorities to better provide them with support to attract additional FDI. Such support includes coordinating activities between local and central governments, developing entrepreneurship, and removing obstacles to FDI.

Urban Governance and Sector-Relevant Institutions

Urban governance reflects Uzbekistan's highly centralized nature, with a dominance of national-level institutions over deconcentrated levels of government at the regional and subregional levels. With the exception of the capital city, municipal administrations, including large cities, report to regional governors and do not have separate budgetary control nor independent decision-making powers. The limited degree of deconcentration and the lack of decentralization act as a hurdle to urban development, to successful local economies, and to the livability of Uzbek cities.

[26]   United Nations Conference on Trade and Development. 2019. *World Investment Report 2019: Special Economic Zones.* Geneva.
[27]   Organisation for Economic Co-operation and Development. 2019. *Sustainable Infrastructure for Low-carbon Development in Central Asia and the Caucasus: Hotspot Analysis and Needs Assessment.*
[28]   Government of Uzbekistan, Ministry of Investment and Foreign Trade. 2020. *Free Economic Zones.* Tashkent. 8 May.

Central Government Institutions

Urban governance involves several central government ministries, agencies, departments, and committees, as well as subnational administrations, or khokimyats. The current process of institutional reform generates some conflicting mandates among the departments as to the attribution of responsibilities and roles. The five most relevant ministries for the urban sector are the following:

- The Ministry of Economic Development and Poverty Reduction promotes and coordinates the national urbanization policy and its implementation, and coordinates the formulation of sectoral and territorial development programs.[29]

- The Ministry of Finance determines the budgets allocated to regions and municipalities and for urban investments in general, including the ones supported by international financial institutions (IFIs).

- The Ministry of Investments and Foreign Trade coordinates the formulation and implementation of development and investment programs, including FDIs, and leads coordination with IFIs.

- The Ministry of Construction formulates and approves urban master plans and other planning instruments, and the enforcement of building codes.

- The Ministry of Housing and Communal Services (MHCS) operates a special fund for housing and communal services, and is responsible for policies and strategies in water supply, sanitation, and district heating systems, and the maintenance of the existing housing stock.

Other relevant ministries and agencies are the State Committee on Land Resources, Geodesy, Cartography and State Cadaster;[30] Ministry of Transport; State Committee on Tourism Development; Ministry of Energy; State Committee for Ecology and Environment Protection; Ministry of Information Technology and Communications; Ministry of Culture; Agency for the Management of State Assets; Agency for the development of public–private partnership under the Ministry of Finance; Ministry of Healthcare, State Sanitary and Epidemiological Service; and Ministry of Emergency Situations.

Multiple state-owned enterprises report to the ministries and agencies listed here, and are responsible for the construction, operation, and maintenance of urban infrastructure and for the delivery of urban services (Section 6). A summary description of the responsibilities of the sector-relevant institutions listed here is presented in Appendix 3.

Regional and Local Government Institutions

Uzbekistan's governance is partially decentralized. Subnational governments (SNGs) act as the central government's agents in the regions. SNGs are accountable to the central government. Authority is delegated to the governors of the regions, who are directly appointed by Presidential Decree.[31] District heads and municipal mayors or khokims are appointed by the regional governors, to whom they report, and preside over public councils composed of locally elected councilors.

---

[29] This Ministry replaced the Ministry of Economy and Industry (MOEI) in March 2020. The former Urbanization Agency under MOEI was replaced by the Department for the Implementation of Urbanization Policies.

[30] Since early September 2020, responsibilities for the state cadaster have been assigned to a newly established Cadaster Agency under the State Tax Commission. Cadastral functions for rural land have been transferred to the Ministry of Agriculture. The Cadaster Agency aims to manage a national cadaster geographic information system containing all cadastral information.

[31] Izvorski, I. et al. 2019. *Uzbekistan Public Expenditure Review*. Washington, DC: World Bank.

Governors report to the President and coordinate the programs of the line ministries and agencies in their respective regions. The capital city, Tashkent, has a status similar to a region, and its mayor is appointed by the President. A certain degree of formal autonomy is given to the Republic of Karakalpakstan, whose Chairman of the Parliament is elected by its legislative assembly, but at the proposal of the President of Uzbekistan, given the Republic's full economic dependence on the country.

Municipalities mainly play a consultative role in implementing investment programs carried out by SOEs and line ministries in the urban space, and act as the linkage between regional governments and communities. Neighborhood or Mahalla Committees are formally established structures that ensure social control by reporting to municipal authorities.

The legislative basis that determines the status of municipalities is Law No. 913 – XII "on municipalities,"dated 2 September 1993, which has been updated by Presidential Decree No. 2497 of 24 February 2016 and by the Decree of the Cabinet of Ministers No. 123 dated 27 April 2016 "on advancement of management structures of regional municipalities." On 9 February 2019, the government issued Presidential Decree No. 4546 "on further reduction of bureaucratic barriers and implementation of modern management principles." Other relevant normative texts include the Decree of the Cabinet of Ministers No. 396 (13 May 2019) "on *hokimiyats*' guarantees on overdue loans taken by homeowners' associations" and Law No. 589 (9 December 2019), National Budget 2020, giving more financial freedom to *hokimiyats* (Section II.2). Appendix 4 has a detailed review of their legal underpinnings.

Intergovernmental Finances

In Uzbekistan, there is no law regulating the functional assignments and administrative sharing between levels of government. While the general divisions of responsibility are specified in the yearly Budget Law, these are not clearly defined and may change during the annual budget process. The deconcentrated expenditure responsibilities assigned to the regions, districts, and cities include social spending (education, health, and social support) and other outlays, but they involve specific task assignments rather than permanent, functional responsibilities (footnote 31). For example, the budget code explicitly specifies that only maintenance and renovation of health-care facilities are the responsibility of SNGs. In education, various levels of government (republic, region, district, city) are all involved in delivering secondary school services. Unclear functional assignments undermine local accountability and efficiency of expenditure and service delivery (footnote 31).

SNGs are currently responsible for about a third of total public expenditure covering general public service; defense; public order and safety; economic affairs; environment; housing and communal services; health, recreation, culture and religion; education; and social protection (Figure 3). The largest allocations go to education (43%), health care (21%), and general public services (15%). Housing and communal services benefit from under 5% of the allocations, confirming the limited attention and resources devoted to urban livability and quality of life.

SNGs generate about 20% of total government revenues in terms of tax collected including, for a minor part, taxes generated locally. These include taxes on property and land, and income from rental, advertising, and motor vehicles sales. Fees are also a source of revenue including those from trading licenses, registrations as a legal entity or entrepreneur, parking fees, motor transport, and development fees.

Individual property taxes, land taxes, and income from rental as part of local fiscal impositions are fully credited to the budgets of cities and districts while corporate property taxes go to regional budgets. The cadastral value determines the property tax base. Individual properties are taxed at variable rates ranging from 0.2% for residences to 2% for properties that have productive purposes. Properties of companies or other legal entities are taxed at 2%.

Figure 3: Subnational Governments' Expenditure as a Percentage
of Total Public Expenditure and Gross Domestic Product, 2011–2019

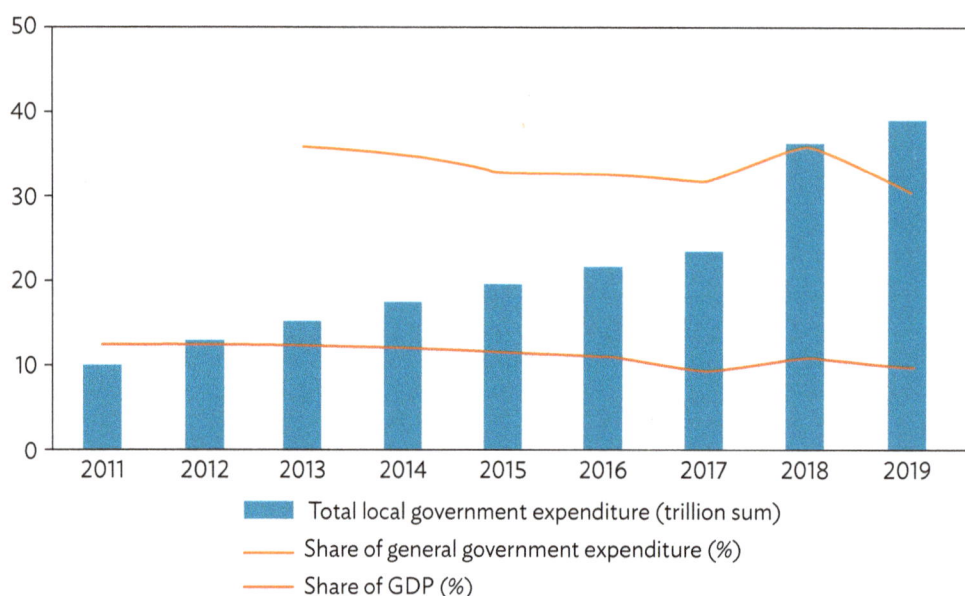

GDP = gross domestic product.
Source: World Bank. 2019. *Uzbekistan Public Expenditure Review.*

The gap between SNG-generated revenues and expenditures is met via central government transfers, which account for about 70% of total SNG revenues. This set up is viewed critically including by the World Bank, which suggested that the balanced budget rule is a key criterion in determining tax sharing rates and the size of targeted social transfers. This balanced budget rule with the budget gap being filled by transfers from the central government does not create local accountability and efficiency in the use of resources. Such approach may underestimate revenues and overestimate spending.

The parameters for both revenues and expenditures are decided annually. The tax sharing types and rates, the amount of targeted transfers, and the number of receiving regions vary across years, which creates uncertainty for local governments (footnote 31).

The absence of rule-based and transparent transfer system can lead to inefficient public financial management, according to the World Bank. The ad hoc approach to resource allocation may translate to these drawbacks:

(i)   The transfer is likely to be influenced by political manipulation.
(ii)   SNGs are perceived as a lower priority and more likely to experience reduction when fiscal retrenchment is needed.
(iii) The link between expenditure responsibilities and revenue resources is broken, which can negatively affect the level of service delivery.
(iv)   Subnational governments are likely to be discouraged from increasing efficiency (footnote 31).

Currently, the human resources of municipalities, perhaps with the exception of the capital city, have insufficient qualified staff to take on further responsibilities and evolve toward a more sophisticated urban management system. For instance, the World Bank, in its project appraisal document for its Medium-Size Cities Integrated

Urban Development Project, states that "many municipalities are lacking a systematic approach toward asset management and need the right software equipment for asset management (e.g., geographic information system [GIS]-based systems) and/or training of municipal officials in the use of those systems."[32]

Urban Real-Estate Management and Urban Planning

The ownership of urban land has so far remained public, although legal reforms for its privatization are underway (Part II, Section 2). At independence in 1991, Uzbekistan's land assets, both rural and urban, were owned by the government, as well as residential buildings, except for rural housing units, which are predominantly "occupier-owned" even during Soviet Union times. The government privatized the residential properties between 1991 and 1993, allowing almost 5 million citizens to purchase the housing units they were occupying. The property transfer cost of these privatized units was a fraction of the median wage, and high inflation further reduced the value of individual payments, staggered over several years. Homeownership was thus generalized and has by now been achieved by 95% of the population (footnote 5).

The tenants of multi-story housing blocks became the owners of their apartments. The surfaces of the communal areas were subdivided by the number of housing units and attributed proportionally. The maintenance of the communal areas initially remained the responsibility of the public companies that were already in charge of it, and households compensated them for such services. Subsequent reforms established homeowner associations, which are currently in charge of maintenance of communal areas, including the grounds surrounding the buildings.[33] While these homeowner associations are non-profit, nongovernment organizations established to operate communal services on behalf of its members, in reality, they substantially depend on both local authorities and the MHCS.

The privatization of the housing stock has created a partial real-estate market and incentivized the construction industry, which represented 6.5% of GDP in 2019.[34] A formal mortgage system facilitates the purchase of housing units. Ownership status and transactions are recorded by the State Committee on Land Resources, Geodesy, Cartography and State Cadaster, established in 2004. The Cadaster has digitized many of its records in GIS and is leading efforts to integrate various spatial information layers including for buildings, land units, roads, gas lines, and other utility systems. This data is managed by a total of 17 ministries and agencies, and efforts are being made to create one national GIS database. However, many utilities and agencies, such as in the water supply sector, still lack GIS data and asset mapping capabilities for their operational needs. Since 2014, the cadastral databases have been integrated with the property tax registers as well.

Land-use and urban planning are the responsibilities of the Ministry of Construction, which oversees the activities of the City Architecture Council. This agency monitors the enforcement of and compliance with the laws and regulations related to urban planning and building codes. Urban master plans and project development plans are developed by three separate entities:

- State Unitary Enterprise (SUE) Expertise of Urban Planning Documentation organizes urban planning documentation and advances architectural and spatial planning.
- O'zdavyerloyiha Agency (Research and Design Institute) is involved in city master plan development, primarily in identifying urban land use.
- SUE O'zshaxarsozlik LITI is mandated to assist in the development and issuance of master plans for all regions in Uzbekistan, except for Tashkent.

---

32   World Bank. 2018. *Medium-Size Cities Integrated Urban Development Project*. Washington, DC. 21 November.
33   United Nations Economic Commission for Europe. 2015. *Country Profiles in Housing and Land Management—Uzbekistan*. Geneva.
34   The State Committee of Republic of Uzbekistan on Statistics. 2020. *National Accounts* (accessed 1 May 2020).

Master plans for cities with a population under 100,000 are approved by the Ministry, while those for the larger cities require the approval of the Cabinet of Ministers.

Current urban planning for the cities in Uzbekistan is however limited to architectural urban design solutions. Little attention is given to productive and welfare opportunities, public spaces, integration of urban infrastructure systems into urban fabrics, and density. According to the Center for Economic Research, master plans should be based on elaborated strategies of urban social and economic development and should determine the long-term prospects of city development as well as the driving forces that will be the basis for the city's future economic growth.[35]

Housing

The urban housing sector is characterized by an aging and ill-maintained stock, insufficient supply to meet the demographic growth of demand and potential further rural to urban migration, and very low affordability, particularly in Tashkent. The housing stock consisted of 5.7 million dwellings in 2015. Single-family homes show a prevalence of 70% in urban areas, followed by apartment buildings which is 30% of the total housing units. Given the average size of the Uzbek household of 5.3 people, a typical apartment consists of four rooms, with an average total size of 80 square meters (m^2). Around 30% of the current housing stock is over 50 years old, built prior to 1970; another 30% was built between 1970 and 1990; and the rest, 40%, is under 30 years old. Today, a key challenge is access to high-quality and reliable communal services and energy efficient housing.

The building characteristics of urban single-family homes consist of a courtyard layout, a one- or two-story construction, the use of bricks or cement blocks for walls, and metal-sheeting for roofing. Apartment buildings do not generally surpass four- or five-story heights on account of anti-seismic building risks. They have flat roofs, and have been erected with reinforced concrete structure and brick walls, sometimes with the use of prefabricated concrete panels. Housing blocks are regrouped into housing estates, with some onsite facilities and communal grounds that surround the buildings, which in general, are badly maintained or in a state of disrepair.

State ownership of urban land is considered a major disincentive for the construction of additional housing units, which occurs at a low yearly rate of 1.9 units per 1,000 inhabitants. Comparator countries present higher housing growth rates, such as Belarus and the Russian Federation with 5.5 units per 1,000 inhabitants, and Kazakhstan with 3.3 units per 1,000 inhabitants. Uzbekistan's current housing supply is well below the estimated demand, amid the current low rate of urbanization.

Uzshahar Qurilish Invest LLC is the national developer that receives most of the government's subsidies to the housing sector. The citizens who receive such subsidy through the developer must be approved by the Mahalla Committees to acquire mortgages to repay the cost of the housing unit over time. However, the great majority of new units were self-financed and only 9,000 to 20,000 mortgages per year were issued between 2010 and 2020.[36]

[35]   Center for Economic Research. 2009. Urbanization and Industrialization in Uzbekistan: Challenges, Problems and Prospects. *Policy Brief* 2009/01. Tashkent. This study reviewed master plans developed in 2008 for Bukhara, Navoi, Termez, Namangan, Nukus, and Zarafshan cities.

[36]   ADB. 2018. *Mortgage Market Development Program—Housing Policy and Subsidy Component.* Consultant's report. Manila (TA 9479-UZB).

The Ministry of Construction programs added around 10,000 to 16,000 new units per year over the last decade, through the Young Family Program, which started in 2007 and the Rural Housing Program, which started in 2009 and was reformed in 2017. The Urban Affordable Housing Program was also launched in 2017. Uzbekistan has a small public rental housing stock (around 40,000 units) for poor households at highly subsidized rents and located mostly in urban areas (footnote 36).

Overall, sector studies point to an estimated housing production of 90,000 units per year between 2010 and 2020 (assuming an average of 80 m^2 per unit). Public sector developers commissioned most of the residential construction, but private individuals are becoming increasingly active in housing production, which is considered a safe and profitable investment in inflationary times. About 100,000 new housing units per year will be established up to 2040, with an upper estimate of 125,000 housing units. Uzbekistan would also need an additional new 45,000 units per year until 2040 to address its accumulated housing deficit and to improve living conditions while decreasing overcrowding.

In summary, Uzbekistan needs to produce upward from 145,000 new housing units per year for the next 25 years to deal with new household formation and poor existing housing conditions, with the majority in urban areas. Despite the government's efforts to address the gaps in housing, the demand overwhelmingly surpasses the supply, and the housing shortfall continues to rise annually. Meanwhile, the quality of the existing housing stock needs improvement and maintenance (footnote 36).

The MHCS is in charge of the governance and maintenance of the existing privatized multifamily housing stock, which is implemented through homeowner associations. These, however, find it difficult to maintain six building blocks on average (approximately 190 units) assigned to them, as apartment owners tend to earn below-average incomes. Consequently, many buildings need bigger and more expensive repairs (footnote 36).

Housing affordability compounds the problems of insufficient supply and low maintenance of the housing stock. The World Bank reports that rent was on average 2.5 times higher in Uzbekistan's urban areas than in rural areas in 2018, and the cost of living is most dramatically higher in the city of Tashkent (footnote 5). On the other hand, rent prices in regions like Syrdarya are as low as 5% of the rent pricing in the capital.

The cost of living in Andijan is 181% of the national average; Samarkand is at 226% while the city of Tashkent is at 550%, according to a World Bank report. These figures were calculated after adjusting for housing characteristics. In urban areas, the average rent expenses accounted for more than 28% of consumption. About 45% of urban households allocated more than 30% of their budget into housing, which is internationally considered the threshold of housing affordability. In the most expensive urban market of Tashkent, rent prices were more than 47% of total average consumption in 2018 (footnote 5).

Although most of the households in Tashkent earn the highest average incomes in the country, more than 72% of them could not afford a housing unit if they did not own it. The thin supply of rental housing and high rental prices are largely due to a high ownership rate (95% of the people in Uzbekistan own their units). In the early 1990s, after its independence, Uzbekistan largely privatized dwellings (but not land) that were formerly publicly owned. The government allowed people who occupied dwellings to purchase them at a low cost. The current market prices, however, are unaffordable, even exclusionary, for those who wish to move into the city. The cost of moving, especially to the capital and to regional cities, is also high. The unaffordable market therefore tends to slow the pace of urbanization (footnote 5). The World Bank reports that in 2018, the median wage in Tashkent city was 61% higher than the national average, and 88% higher than among those employed in rural areas.

Urban Infrastructure and Services

Capital investments and operations and maintenance of infrastructure and services delivery are currently the responsibility of line ministries and regional governments but are mostly carried out by public utility companies that control the assets and the delivery of services. Overall, there has been a decline in the levels of service in the past decades due to aging assets mostly built in Soviet Union times, the inefficient systems of service provision and operations and maintenance, ad hoc tariffs that were insufficient for cost recovery, slow-evolving sector and utility governance, and limited cost recovery.

Water Supply and Sanitation

Water supply and sanitation (WSS) infrastructure in the country failed to stay up-to-date with urban demand and industrial needs due to financial and institutional difficulties that the WSS sector experienced after independence. Asset bases rapidly became obsolete, resulting in high leakage losses and increased water pollution. Consequently, service continuity and expanding water supply access have become one of the government's main priorities. To increase water access and ensure service continuity and efficiency, efforts to construct and reconstruct water treatment plants, pipelines, pumping stations, and distribution systems have been conducted. Water conservation is one of the pillars of these efforts, among other institutional and operational reforms.

During 1991–2012, more than 54,000 kilometers (km) of trunk mains and pipelines were reportedly constructed, including over 48,000 km in rural areas. During 2005–2010, utility water coverage increased from 69% to 73%. However, despite a strong sustainability focus and relatively high overall network coverage, water supply indicators show mixed sector performance. Water supply disruptions are common, with many urban consumers suffering supply limitations. Average non-revenue water (NRW) is currently estimated at 29%; though with limited metering, it is difficult to measure NRW precisely. In individual cities, however, NRW can reach around 60% due to aging infrastructure and poor operation and maintenance.[37]

Out of the 32.1 million people in Uzbekistan, only 20.7 million (64.5% of the population) are served by centralized water supply. In fact, 13.5 million people (42% of the population) have in-house connections to water supply networks while 7 million people (22% of the population) are serviced by standpipes on the street. On the other hand, close to 8 million people (25% of the population) are left to use alternative sources of water supply such as springs, wells, rivers, and other natural sources. Around 3.3 million people (10.3% of the population) depend on water delivered by trucks.

Approximate figures show that less than 20% of the population is connected to centralized sewerage systems. As of 2017, such systems were available in only 79 cities and towns, where sewerage systems were provided to about half of the households.

Although systems are generally designed with mechanical structures (sand traps and septic tanks), biological treatment (aeration), effluent disinfection (chlorination), and partial sludge treatment (aerobic stabilization, drying of sludge on sites), reports indicate that many may not meet the prescribed treatment standards (footnote 37).

---

[37]   ADB. 2019. *Report and Recommendation of the President to the Board of Directors: Proposed Loan to the Republic of Uzbekistan for the Second Tashkent Province Water Supply Development Project.* Manila.

While infrastructure gaps persist, the sustainable operation, maintenance, and management of such physical investments remain a huge challenge. Infrastructure development should be complemented with institutional development to facilitate cost recovery tariffs, performance-based service contracts, and public–private partnerships (PPPs). Capacity of utilities should be built, coupled with stronger human resource management and incentives to improve worker motivations and accountability. Modernization through automated digital systems of technical and financial controls will also efficiently facilitate asset management, customer grievances, and billing and collection.

The open discharge of industrial chemicals into sewers and waterways, particularly textile dyes in Tashkent, create environmental risks, as well as operational risks to existing sewage treatment plants not designed to treat such chemicals. Stronger pollution control measures are therefore required.

Solid Waste Management

In Uzbekistan, more than 12,000 tons of municipal solid waste are generated each day, which results in over 4.4 million tons per year. These figures are expected to go up to 18,000 tons per day and 6.6 million tons per year by 2035. Recycling is not regulated and is rather improvised by self-organized waste-picker groups in some sites. Regular collection services are limited to 30% of the population while the remaining 70% is not served, and is left to organize its own collection service or to dump waste within the community. There are 296 disposal sites that pose great stress on the environment and on public health.[38]

Solid waste management (SWM) services are not equally provided in every municipality, many of which find it increasingly challenging to serve communities due to funding constraints (low public funding and minimal tariffs). With the exception of Tashkent City, throughout the country, service delivery is weak. Regulatory and institutional frameworks that will facilitate compliance, accountability, and efficient enforcement are lacking. Opportunities for private sector participation in SWM are also being missed. Ultimately, this translates into urban–rural access inequalities, environmental degradation, public health threats, and as a consequence, constrained economic growth (footnote 38).

District Heat Supply

Operations of district heating companies (DHCs) become unviable due to heat tariffs that are below cost recovery levels and because of low heat bill collection rates. DHCs also suffer from high network heat and water losses, poor operational management, and under-investments in rehabilitation of main assets.[39]

Prior to Uzbekistan's independence, district heating services such as space heating and hot water were provided to most urban settlements by public sector companies owned by municipalities. There are now 33 DHCs managed by the MHCS, established in April 2017. Most district heating assets date back to the 1950s or 1970s, which explains their current precarious state. Legacy deficiencies such as energy inefficient open systems for hot water supply and under-funding of DHCs for maintenance, rehabilitation, and modernization have shaped Uzbekistan's current district heating capacity. Additionally, DHCs struggle to operate with below-cost-recovery tariffs, low heat bill collection rates, and poor operational management. Tashkent has the largest district heating system in the country and represents 70% of the country's overall district heating services provision. All other cities have lost the practice of investments in operation and maintenance of the district heating infrastructure.

---

38   ADB. 2019. *Republic of Uzbekistan: Proposed Sustainable Solid-Waste Management Project—Concept Paper.* Manila.
39   World Bank. 2018. *Project Appraisal Document: District Heating Energy Efficiency Project.* Washington, DC.

Consequently, citizens have opted to use electricity and gas to heat spaces and water in multi-apartment and public buildings, resulting in

(i)   inefficient use of electricity and natural gas due to wide usage of crude devices;
(ii)   overloaded power sector assets, which cause accelerated wear and tear and consequently, frequent power outages, especially during winter; and
(iii)   safety and health risks that stem from the use of poor-quality or polluting heaters and stoves.

In general, a key issue is the low energy efficiency of housing, including some of the newly constructed buildings. There are two main factors that are crucial to the development of future urban and rural housing and office buildings: (i) introduction of a transparent and clear system of commissioning, and (ii) introduction of a tariff for heating with simultaneous change from "normative-based billing" to ubiquitous introduction of metering.

These risks disproportionately affect household members who are primarily responsible for carrying out energy-related tasks, such as women in charge of household tasks; men and women using faulty or poor-quality electric, gas, and coal heaters and stoves; and elderly family members spending a large amount of time at home (footnote 39).

Electricity and Gas

Uzbekistan is 100% electrified, but service quality is poor and unreliable. The country's energy infrastructure was mostly constructed during the Soviet Union era. The electricity transmission and distribution lines are on average about 30 years old, and this aging infrastructure has been largely the cause of inefficient and unreliable energy supply in the country. According to a World Bank report, gas supply losses are estimated to be more than 30% of production, and electricity losses around 20% of net generation.[40] Gas losses are more than 15 times, and electricity losses about three times the average losses in Organisation for Economic Co-operation and Development (OECD) countries (footnote 40).

Demand for power in Uzbekistan has increased with a high upsurge that begun in 2010 driven by the industry and residential sectors. However, the aging power infrastructure and insufficient investment have widened the supply–demand gap and resulted in supply reliability issues. Unreliable power supply has negatively affected people's livelihoods and business profitability. According to the World Bank Enterprise Survey 2019, electrical outages of 2.3 hours happen twice a month. Losses because of outages amount to 3.0% of annual sales of enterprises, which is higher than the average for Eastern Europe and Central Asia. The issues are acute in rural and remote areas, putting social services such as schools and clinics at risk during the winter seasons when electricity demand hikes. Gender analysis highlights that unstable and low-quality electricity disproportionately affects women, who are primary users of household electricity. More reliable electricity will improve women's well-being and socioeconomic condition and increase opportunities for them to participate in productive works.[41]

The World Bank describes Uzbekistan as one of the most energy-intensive countries in the world. Although the country's energy use declined by 45% during 1998–2013, its energy use per unit of GDP is more than three times the average of energy use by countries in the Europe and Central Asia region. In Uzbekistan, metallurgy, cement, and chemicals industries still operate the most electricity-intensive technologies. The outdated equipment and technologies and lack of incentives for energy savings have resulted in demand-side inefficiencies. Increased

---

40   World Bank. 2019. *Sustaining Market Reforms in Uzbekistan Development Policy Operation*. Washington, DC.
41   ADB. 2020. *Proposed Programmatic Approach and Policy-Based Loan for Subprogram 1: Republic of Uzbekistan Power Sector Reform Program— Concept Paper*. Manila.

climate variability and extreme weather events are expected to put further pressure on the country's energy system (footnote 40).

Implementing policies to improve energy efficiency will be necessary to meet the country's commitments under the Paris Agreement. Based on the promising outcome of ADB-funded advanced electricity metering project, the government launched on 20 August 2020 an ADB-funded smart electricity metering data center, which was successfully completed in 2020. By 2022, the nationwide smart metering program will be completed and the center will process electricity consumption and billing information from 7 million smart meters across the country. The government commenced a program to roll out a smart gas metering program. Smart metering will improve energy efficiency and the sector's sustainability and provide better services for consumers.

The financial situation of electricity and gas energy utilities in the country has been weakened by limited loss reductions, ad-hoc tariff adjustments and pricing policy, and poor collection rates. This was compounded by foreign exchange debt exposure following the September 2017 devaluation of the som. These utilities received government budgetary support to cover foreign exchange losses post-devaluation, while also being subject to the government's plans to strengthen financial and operational transparency (footnote 40). Inadequate billing and metering systems and a low tariff policy exacerbate the situation by encouraging wasteful electricity consumption. Without substantial tariff adjustments, the sector's performance will deteriorate further. While cost recovery tariff setting and enforcement are required for the sustainability of the sector, social acceptance and safeguard measures for vulnerable households also need to be in place.

Urban Roads, Public Spaces, and Transport Systems

Construction and maintenance of urban roads is the responsibility of municipalities, to which they devote part of their limited infrastructure and communal services budget. In the absence of a systematic survey or data on the state of the urban road networks in Uzbekistan's cities, anecdotal evidence points to the pre-eminence of primary trunk roads and the scarcity of secondary and tertiary roads. Primary roads are generally laid-out as wide or very wide multiple carriageway arteries, linking important intersections and monumental urban landmarks. They tend to be well-maintained, are buffered by landscaped areas, and provide the iconic public urban image, a vision of monumental urban design that the center of Uzbek cities share with all post-Soviet Union urban centers.

The network thins out considerably when moving off the main arteries into secondary and tertiary roads leading into and through low-density residential neighborhoods. Maintenance is lacking; paving gives way to uneven, unpaved streets, generally without drainage infrastructure, causing stagnating water and potholes; and street lighting is equally scarce. Housing estates enclose their own internal streets and open spaces, suffering from even worse neglect and lack of maintenance.

No data was available on the planning, consistency, and state of maintenance of public spaces in Uzbekistan's cities. Anecdotal evidence points to a significant discrepancy between the planned parks and landscaped areas adjacent to important public buildings and monuments, and the neighborhood-level open spaces. The latter suffers from neglect, which consist mostly of residual areas that could not be urbanized or built upon, and do not appear to benefit from systematic maintenance. As mentioned in the previous section on housing, open areas contained within the boundaries of housing estates are subject to the financial resource limitations constraining the estates' upkeep.

Urban transport in Uzbekistan is limited to buses and minibuses, and the metro system in Tashkent city. Low public transportation coverage and options has led to the significant growth of private vehicle use, mostly for single persons. Urban transport in Tashkent has experienced a dramatic transformation. The city's tram network was first established in 1896, buses were introduced in 1909, public taxis in 1937, and the metro system was built in 1971, when Tashkent had a population of 1 million. At independence, Tashkent had a total of 288 km of tram rails, 300 km of trolleybus routes, with related rolling stock, depots and maintenance yards, 2 underground metro lines with 23 stations, 2,243 buses on 128 routes, and a fleet of 3,355 taxis.[42]

The shift to individual motorization included the termination of the trolleybus system in 2010, followed by the termination of the tram system in 2016—by then reduced to 90 km—making way to further widening of roads for more cars. The production of Daewoo (formerly General Motors) motorcars in Andijan since 1996 has supported the gradual replacement of public transport by private vehicles. In 2009, registered cars in Tashkent were 300,000. The construction of the two ring roads and various tunnels and bridges, along with the liberalization of taxi services, have accelerated individual motorization; and many private cars now double up as freelance taxis. By 2019, Tashkent had 406,000 registered cars, 500 official taxis, and only 500 standard and 200 small buses.[43] Currently, Tashkent city administration supports the introduction of e-bus and e-taxi based vehicles, 300 in total, to become operational in 2021. Trial e-buses have been put into operation on selected routes in Tashkent since early 2020.

The state of urban transport systems in secondary cities is underdeveloped. Official reports are not publicly accessible, and donor agencies have not been involved since the seminal ADB study of 2006 and the World Bank Urban Transport Project of 2000.[44] The ADB study reports, among other things, on the incomplete construction of the third Tashkent metro line and on the small trolleybus systems still operating at the time in Almalyk, Bukhara, Djizzak, Fergana, Namangan, Nukus, and Urgench.

A World Bank operation supported the cities of Almalyk, Bukhara, Namangan, Nukus, and Samarkand with (i) increased supply of urban passenger transport services to satisfy demand, (ii) management of transport operations and maintenance of vehicles by transport operators, (iii) allocation of bus routes franchises on the basis of competitive bidding process, (iv) planning of urban transport systems and administration of franchise contracts, and (v) enabling the urban transport operators in the five cities to fully recover their costs.

Urban Environment and Livability

Uzbek cities suffer from overall low livability due to a number of factors, including (i) insufficient formal job opportunities and low wages, (ii) former constraints to free mobility and to private ownership of land, (iii) poor housing conditions, and (iv) insufficient provision of urban infrastructure and key related services, as reported in the previous sections. Urban livability is also negatively impacted by unexpected shocks, such as COVID-19, limited natural resources, poor urban environmental quality and public health, and high exposure of Uzbek cities to natural hazards and climate change risks.

Limited Natural Resources

While some Uzbek cities are affected by low water supply, most cities struggle with providing sufficient drinking water due to poor operation and maintenance of existing resources and infrastructure, high NRW levels, and poor management. Currently, water scarcity ranges around 13% to 14% of demand, but could reach 44% to 46%

[42]   A. Akimov and D. Banister. 2011. Urban Transport in Post-Communist Tashkent. *Comparative Economic Studies*. 53. pp. 721–755.
[43]   J. M. Grütter and K. J. Kim. 2019. E-Mobility Options for ADB Developing Member Countries. *ADB Sustainable Development Working Paper Series No. 60*. Manila: ADB.
[44]   ADB. 2006. *Uzbekistan: Transport Sector Strategy 2006–2020*. Manila.

by 2030 if mitigation and adaptation measures are not successfully implemented. If water for irrigation is not available, agriculture will take a toll in the amount of jobs it can sustain, which could also lead to greater migration from rural to urban areas. There is also a need to introduce innovative methods for reducing NRW in urban distribution networks and in the irrigation sector.

Central Asia's wide mountain ranges are the origin of most of the region's water resources. Tajikistan holds 40% and the Kyrgyz Republic 30% of the water resources serving the five Central Asia countries.[45] Uzbekistan receives 90% of its water from these mountains and is therefore highly dependent on these resources. The Fergana Valley relies on water bodies located in the Kyrgyz Republic and Tajikistan; Tashkent and the Fergana Valley face risks of flooding due to glacial lake outbursts in the surrounding mountainous areas; Karakalpakstan might be affected by drought due to erratic rain patterns; the Rogun Dam project on the Vakhsh River in Tajikistan, financed by the World Bank, will impact the flow of the Amu Darya river by 29% (20 billion cubic meters);[46] and consequently, irrigation of Uzbek cotton fields might be negatively impacted.[47]

The World Health Organization (WHO) points to the Karakalpakstan region as one of the most affected by accelerated desertification, driven by water shortage, climate change, and land degradation.[48] Social problems persist in Karakalpakstan and the Khorezm Province as a result of increasing water scarcity in the region.[49] Water scarcity in the Khorezm region is attributed to the desiccation of the Aral Sea and its harmful impacts on the Amu Darya river flow, especially around the Priaralie, littoral zone of the Aral Sea.[50] The region's once prosperous fishing industry has been ravaged, bringing unemployment and economic hardship.

Urban Environmental Quality and Public Health

Waterborne diseases play a major role in Uzbekistan's public health. The World Bank estimated that in 2012 only 17% of urban households had access to running water 24 hours a day.[51] In many urban outskirts and rural areas, wastewater does not find its way into a central sewerage system and may be disposed of directly into the environment without any treatment. Additionally, water pollution from industrial wastes and the heavy use of fertilizers and pesticides are the cause of many human health disorders. Public health is at risk due to recurrent leakages of collectors or networks and uncontrolled discharge of wastewater into urban centers like Khodjeyli and others, where the wastewater management system lacks the infrastructure to serve the resident population.[52]

Drinking water resources that originate from the Zarafshan river are polluted from industrial enterprises that are discharging sewage waters in populated areas, including in the city of Samarkand and into farmland reservoirs. The high level of contamination of the Zarafshan along the sleeve of the Karadarya and the Siab collector is the result of discharges from sewage treatment plants and poorly managed city drainage systems.[53]

45   University of Central Asia, et al. 2012. *Sustainable Mountain Development in Central Asia. From Rio 1992 to 2012 and Beyond.*
46   World Bank. 2014. *Key Issues for Consideration on the Proposed Rogun Hydropower Project.* Washington, DC.
47   Environment Conflict and Cooperation Platform. 2020. *Rogun Dam Conflict between Tajikistan and Uzbekistan.*
48   World Health Organization. 2016. *Climate Change Adaptation to Protect Human Health.*
49   M. Kļaviņš, A. Azizov, and J. Zaļoksnis. 2014. *Environment, Pollution, Development: The Case of Uzbekistan.* Tashkent.
50   Government of Uzbekistan, Ministry of Foreign Affairs. 2018. *About Aral, Time and Again.*
51   World Bank. 2015. *The Case of Uzbekistan: Social Impact Analysis of Water Supply and Sanitation Services in Central Asia.* Washington, DC.
52   Government of Uzbekistan, Ministry of Housing and Communal Services. 2020. *Water Services and Institutional Support Program.*
53   ADB. 2019. *Report and Recommendation of the President to the Board of Directors: Proposed Loan to the Republic of Uzbekistan for the Sustainable Solid-Waste Management Project.* Manila.

The shrinkage of the Aral Sea has resulted in growing concentrations of chemical pesticides and natural salts, which are then blown from the increasingly exposed lake bed and contribute to desertification and respiratory health problems.[54] Dust with high levels of toxicity often travel long distances and accumulate in rural and urban settlements.

Air pollution levels in industrial cities like Almalyk, Andijan, Angren, Bekabad, Bukhara, Chirchik, Fergana, Navoi, Nukus, and Tashkent often exceed health standards. In 2019, for example, Tashkent came in with a yearly particulate matter (PM) 2.5 average reading of 41.2 µg/m³ (one-millionth of a gram per cubic meter air). This placed the city into the "unhealthy for sensitive groups" bracket, which requires a PM2.5 reading of anywhere between 35.5 to 55.4 µg/m³ to be classified as such. Industrial dust affecting urban areas usually originate from the activities of SOEs. Higher specific dust emissions are observed in cities where cement industry and coal-burning powerplants are mostly located.[55] Tashkent scored as the 18th most polluted capital city in the world out of 92 capital cities assessed for the year 2020.[56] Air pollution is associated with the quality of outdoor urban air, but human health may also be affected by indoor air pollution, such as in dwelling and working premises (footnote 55). The indoor use of coal-fueled stoves increases exposure to substances with toxic properties. Around 12% of households in Uzbekistan use solid fuels (especially wood); in rural areas, 25% of the population uses solid fuels, and natural gas is commonly used for cooking. Reportedly, there are 6,200 deaths per year from indoor air pollution and 3,800 from outdoor air pollution.[57]

Natural Hazards and Climate Change Risks

As much as 80.4% of the population in Uzbekistan lives within areas of high or very high seismic hazard. Tashkent, Samarkand, Bukhara, and the Fergana Valley are subject to earthquakes with an intensity of 7 or higher (MSK scale) every 50 years—in the case of Tashkent, 25 years.[58] On 26 April 1966, Tashkent was struck by an earthquake that killed 10 people, affected 100,000 others, and caused an economic loss of $300 million.[59]

Tashkent, Samarkand, and the urban centers of the Surkhandarya and Kashkadarya Regions are vulnerable to landslides due to geodynamic movements, rising water tables, and increasing torrential rainfall, deforestation, and mining activities. In the Fergana Valley, landslides can trigger transboundary hazards like glacial lake outburst floods and the release of toxic substances in river basins. The Sarez lake in the Pamir mountains is at risk of flooding the downstream valley of the Amu Darya River with its 16 cubic kilometers of water if an earthquake ruptures its naturally formed dam (footnote 58).

The Global Facility for Disaster Reduction and Recovery (GFDRR) Innovation Lab found that the annual average population at risk of earthquakes is about 1 million, and the annual average GDP at risk is $2 billion. The projected urbanization rate, aging infrastructure, and demographic growth will accentuate this trend in the absence of risk mitigation.[60] GFDRR supports Uzbekistan's priority to reduce seismic risks, particularly for priority buildings in Tashkent.[61]

---

[54]   Central Intelligence Agency. 2020. *Central Asia: Uzbekistan. Environment—Current Issues.*
[55]   Government of Uzbekistan, Ministry of Foreign Affairs. 2018. *Protection of the Environment is an Important Factor in Ensuring Public Health.*
[56]   IQAir. 2020. *World Air Quality Report: Region & City PM2.5 Ranking.* Switzerland.
[57]   United Nations Environment Programme. 2015. Air Quality Policies.
[58]   J. F. Linn. 2010. Protection Against Severe Earthquake Risks in Central Asia. *Brookings.* 23 March.
[59]   M. Thurman. 2011. *Natural Disaster Risks in Central Asia: A Synthesis.* United Nations Development Programme.
[60]   *World Bank.* 2016. Uzbekistan Moves Towards Proactive Approach to Disaster Risk Management. 14 December.
[61]   Global Facility for Disaster Reduction and Recovery (GFDRR). Uzbekistan.

On account of climate change, heat waves and increased frequency of the consecutive number of days above 39°C are expected to occur throughout the country.[62] Increased temperatures would also affect spring frosts, further worsening the adverse impacts on the agriculture sector. WHO identifies climate-sensitive diseases such as waterborne acute intestinal diseases, and cardiovascular and respiratory diseases that have increased risk during climatic events like droughts and heat waves (footnote 48). Extreme heat hazard is classified as high in Uzbekistan, based on modeled heat information currently available via the ThinkHazard tool.[63] The frequency of extremely hot days (40°C or above) has risen, while recurrence of low temperatures has diminished (footnote 59). In Tashkent, the highest air temperature in July 2018 was 43°C. In 2019, temperatures ranged between 37°C and 40°C, while in the south and the desert zone, temperatures were up to 42°C (footnote 59).

---

[62]   World Bank. Uzbekistan.
[63]   *KUN.UZ.* 2019. Uzbekistan Heatwave Temperatures to Reach 42°C. 8 July.

II. Government Policies and Programs

Urban Development Policies

Urbanization and the National Development Strategy

In February 2017, barely 2 months into office, the new President signed the Decree "on the strategy for the further development of the Republic of Uzbekistan" with a 5-year time horizon to 2021. This foundational document indicated the five priority areas of the reform process: (i) improving state and social construction; (ii) ensuring the rule of law and further reforming the judicial system; (iii) development and liberalization of the economy; (iv) development of the social sphere; and (v) ensuring security, inter-ethnic harmony, and religious tolerance, pursuing a balanced, mutually beneficial, and constructive foreign policy. It was a broad and ambitious statement of intents of a new direction for the country, which the new government embarked on implementing.

The Action Strategy attached to the Decree further articulates the priority areas, including the "integrated and balanced socioeconomic development of regions, districts and cities, the optimal and efficient use of their potential." The government plans to achieve this goal through the following:

- Ensure the integrated and efficient use of natural, mineral and raw materials, industrial, agricultural, tourism and labor potential of each region to accelerate socioeconomic development and increase the level of employment and incomes of the population.

- Reduce the gap in socioeconomic development among the regions by modernizing and diversifying the economy of the territories, accelerating the development of relatively lagging regions and cities, and increasing their industrial and export potential.

- Actively develop small cities and urban-type settlements by creating new industrial enterprises and service centers and small industrial zones, and attracting funds from large business associations, bank loans, and private foreign investments.

- Provide subsidies and support to districts and cities, in view of the expansion of the revenue base of local budgets due to the rapid development of industries and services.

- Further develop and modernize the production, engineering, communication and social infrastructure of the territories to create favorable conditions for industrial and production facilities, foster the broad development of private enterprise, and improve the living conditions of the population.[64]

---

[64] Commonwealth of Independent States (CIS) Legislation. 2019. *Presidential Decree of the Republic of Uzbekistan of 7 February 2017 No. UP-4947 "About the strategy of actions for further development of the Republic of Uzbekistan" (as amended on 10-12-2019).*

Presidential Decree on Urbanization

On 10 January 2019, Presidential Decree No. 5623 "on measures to fundamentally improve the process of urbanization" was signed into law. The Decree has set out goals for an entirely liberalized urban development sector: (i) full private property rights over urban land; (ii) free movement of people from rural to urban areas; (iii) optimizing agglomeration opportunities to provide urban employment; (iv) an expanded provision of housing, urban infrastructure and services, including via proper housing finance; (v) harnessing international know-how for improved urban development; and (vi) expansion of satellite centers in the proximity of cities.

Such goals are to be achieved via several provisions, as specified in the Decree:

- Define procedures for land privatization and compensation via the Cadaster Committee.
- Develop and approve a more detailed urbanization development concept.
- Establish the Agency for Urbanization under the Ministry of Economy and Industry to be in charge of urban policy, territorial development, and the optimal hierarchy of urban centers.
- Create the Urban Development Fund to recoup funding from land privatization and to invest in urban infrastructure and services provision, and support housing finance.
- Identify the land opportunities for urban development via the Ministry of Construction, the Cadaster Committee, and the Agency for Urbanization.
- Improve the quality of urban data via the State Committee on Statistics.
- Develop plans for public housing construction for the 2020–2025 period.
- Approve the Roadmap attached to the Decree which specifies institutional roles and target dates for the implementation of the urban sector reforms.
- Require the Central Bank to modernize procedures for the registration of mortgage loans.
- Require the Ministry of Economy and the Ministry of Justice to regulate the Urban Development Fund.
- Request the national media to publicize the new orientations of urban development.

An ambitious timeline was set for the implementation of most of the above measures, many of which were supposed to take place in 2019. The implementation progress of these urban development reforms is reported in Section 2.

National Development Strategy to 2030

In the National Development Strategy of the Republic of Uzbekistan until 2030, the theme of urbanization and regional development has been further developed by the then Ministry of Economy and Industry, now the Ministry of Economic Development and Poverty Reduction.[65] Although the strategy is already being used as a policy reference, the Council of Ministers has yet to approve it.

In its Section XII on "ensuring sustainable and balanced development of regions," the strategy addresses the current imbalances among Uzbek regions in terms of their contribution to GDP creation as well as the levels of socioeconomic development. A number of measures are proposed to redress such imbalances, including creating new industrial clusters, techno-parks, and free transborder trade zones; diversifying the economic base

---

[65] Government of Uzbekistan, Ministry of Economy and Industry. *National Development Strategy of the Republic of Uzbekistan until 2030.* Unpublished.

of some regions; pursuing further decentralization; and developing regional growth poles. The strategy states the goal of achieving 60% of urbanization by 2030 through implementing the reforms identified in the Decree on Urbanization and preparing a National Strategy for Urbanization to 2030. It also states the government's intention to increase the number of cities from the current 119 to 135 by 2030 via the reclassification of several smaller urban settlements.

Implementation of Reforms and Investment Programs

Creation and Closure of the Urbanization Agency

In May 2019, Uzbekistan's Urbanization Agency was created as an entity that would spearhead the implementation of the new vision for the urban sector as set out by the January 2019 Decree on Urbanization. The Council of Ministers Decree specified the following as the Urbanization Agency's institutional mandates:[66]

- Implement a unified state policy in the sphere of regulation of urbanization processes.
- Conduct long-term planning of rates, stages, and results of industrialization policy; analyze long-term demographic trends in the city and in the countryside; calculate the demographic capacity of cities in the context of rapid industrialization; and calculate the amount of labor requirements in the cities.
- Identify the "growth poles," select the administrative centers, coordinate educational policies, form a labor market, and regulate internal and external migration.
- Develop a comprehensive program to stimulate the movement of labor from villages to cities, and provide institutional measures to organize training of villagers in new industrial specialties.
- Manage the formation of urban agglomerations, taking into account the creation of satellite cities, including the development of social, engineering, communal and road transport infrastructures through the introduction of advanced energy-saving, and environment friendly technologies and materials.
- Regulate the integrated development of the urban system of settlements, and the formation of an effective ratio of small, medium, and large cities, considering international practice.

The responsibilities of the Urbanization Agency include the preparation of the detailed Urbanization Development Concept. While an advanced draft was prepared with ADB's expertise support, as of September 2020, the Concept document had not yet been approved by the President. The draft presents a number of significant and relevant recommendations to address the constraints of the current system of urban development, including a set of detailed solutions, and indicates three possible stages of implementation of the Urbanization Strategy to 2030. The Concept document also flags the urbanization, housing, infrastructure, and service provision quantitative targets to be achieved by 2030.[67]

With the support of ADB and World Bank, the Agency of Urbanization held a policy workshop in September 2019 to lay out the broad guidelines of urban policy development, as its mandate included the coordination and harmonization of the support provided by IFIs. The agency also sought the support of the United Nations Human Settlements Programme (UN Habitat) in establishing urban indicators to be adopted at the national level.

---

[66]   CIS Legislation. 2019. *Resolution of the Cabinet of Ministers of the Republic of Uzbekistan of 31 May 2019 No. 450 "About measures for the organization of activities of the agency of urbanization under the Ministry of Economy and Industry of the Republic of Uzbekistan."*
[67]   Agency for Urbanization. Urbanization Development Concept. Unpublished.

In March 2020, however, the agency was dissolved, signaling a step back in the urban sector reform process. At the same time, the Ministry of Economy and Industry was reorganized into the Ministry of Economic Development and Poverty Reduction. Two departments have since taken over some of the previous functions of the Agency: the Department of Urban Policy, which is responsible for land privatization, urban development, and housing management, and the Department of Road Transport and Communications Infrastructure.

Fiscal Decentralization

One of the core goals of the foundational Presidential Decree of 2017 "on the strategy for the further development of the Republic of Uzbekistan" is reforming "subsidies and support to districts and cities, in view of the expansion of the revenue base of local budgets due to the rapid development in their industry and services." A series of presidential decrees and resolutions were issued in 2017 to support the main objective of the country's budget policy which called for ensuring sustainable finance of the integrated development of territories.

This goal is set to be achieved through (i) radical strengthening of the revenue base and decentralization of local budgets, (ii) further improving inter-budget relations, (iii) strengthening the financial independence of local government bodies, and (iv) increasing their responsibility for implementing specific targeted measures. These measures include expanding the tax potential by promoting the development of small businesses and private enterprises; creating new jobs and ensuring employment of the population; and rapidly developing engineering and communication, road transport, and social infrastructure.[68] The fiscal policy's main directions and priority tasks at the level of local budgets for improving intergovernmental relations are as follows:

(i)   Strengthen the responsibility of local government bodies and financial and tax authorities to increase the revenue base; ensure timely and targeted financing of the approved spending parameters of local budgets; ensure further development and maintenance of social facilities and infrastructure through (a) fixing and/or leaving at their disposal of certain types of taxes and other obligatory payments as the revenues of the local budgets; (b) full coverage of taxpayers on their territory to increase tax collection; (c) creating new production enterprises; and (d) restoring the production activities of economically insolvent, non-working enterprises.

(ii)   On the subvention of provincial, city, and district budgets, consistently reduce their dependence on deductions from higher budgets, increasing on this basis the independence and responsibility of local government bodies in tackling socioeconomic development of the regions.

(iii) Distribute the revenues from certain types of taxes coming from large taxpayers, among the republican budget, local budgets of provinces, and budgets of districts and cities.

(iv)   Provide local authorities with the authority to reduce and increase rates for certain types of local taxes to ensure the uniform development of districts and cities.

(v)   Increase local government autonomy in financing costs for the development of socioeconomic infrastructure and unforeseen expenses.

(vi)   Ensure transparency in the formation and implementation monitoring of local budgets with the wide involvement of deputies and the public control.

The transfer of increased budget powers and responsibilities to local authorities started with the adoption of the State Program on Development Strategy of Uzbekistan (2017–2021). The Strategy envisages expanding the sources of local budget revenues through the sustainable development of sectors and regions, further

---

[68]   Cities Development Initiative for Asia (CDIA). 2020. *Project Preparation Study for the ADB Integrated Urban Development Project in Uzbekistan, Inception Report*. Manila.

optimization of budget expenditures, reduction of subsidies to towns and districts, deepening fiscal decentralization processes, and increasing the transparency of the budgeting process.[69]

On 1 January 2018, measures to strengthen the responsibility of local government bodies and financial and tax authorities were introduced. The responsibilities of and incentives for the heads of financial bodies (including local financial departments) and bodies of the state tax service were laid out. These include bonus payments for achieving the approved forecast of local budget revenues and for reducing tax debt on payments to the budget, and penalties for failure to fulfill the forecast of local budget revenue and the calculated indicators for identifying reserves to increase revenues of local budgets. *Hokims* of provinces, districts, and cities are held personally responsible and strongly advised to ensure the fullness of revenues.

In 2019, local budgets received the right to retain and use the income received in excess of the plan. The course to strengthen local budgets continued in 2020. The 2020 national budget addresses the plans to expand *hokimiyat's* financial self-sufficiency.[70] Since 2020, an income from unified tax payments in full amount, excise tax (mobile networks, alcohol) have been credited to local budgets. Regional governments will be granted with more decision-making power to redistribute their budget.

Public–Private Participation

The Law "About Public–Private Partnership" was approved in May 2019. It sets the stage for public–private partnerships (PPPs), among other things, to assist in "the formation, restoration, operation, maintenance of existing public infrastructure" and improve "the quality of operation and maintenance of public infrastructure." Concessions are valued at a minimum of $1 million and have a duration of 3 to 49 years. The Agency for the Development of Public–Private Partnerships was set up under the Ministry of Finance to promote this agenda and is actively working in this domain, with expertise provided by ADB.

Opportunities for promoting PPPs relevant to urban development include the provision of urban infrastructure and delivery of services such as WSS; PPP studies and transaction advisory services supported by ADB in four cities (Samarkand, Bukhara, Namangan, and Karshi); energy generation; SWM; mass urban transport systems; and housing provision. International experience with PPPs shows varied results. Successful cases point to the presence of regulatory agencies that are able to uphold the terms of the concessions entered into between the public and the private parties, when either one wants to renegotiate the terms.

Privatization of Urban Land Property

On 13 August 2019, the Law "on privatization of non-agricultural land plots" was approved and entered into effect on 1 March 2020.[71] It specifies which types of land plots can be subject to privatization: (i) land plots on which the buildings, structures and industrial infrastructure facilities belonging to legal entities are located, as well as the land adjacent to them to the extent necessary to carry out production activities; (ii) land plots provided to citizens of Uzbekistan for individual housing construction and maintenance of a residential house; (iii) free land plots; and (iv) land plots provided to the Urban Development Fund under the Ministry of Economy and Poverty Reduction.

---

[69]   *CDIA. 2020. Developing Integrated Solutions for Urban Issues in Uzbekistan. 6 April. Manila.*

[70]   CIS Legislation. 2019. *Law of the Republic of Uzbekistan of 9 December 2019 No. ZRU 589 "About the Government budget of the Republic of Uzbekistan for 2020."*

[71]   CIS Legislation. 2019. *Law of the Republic of Uzbekistan of 13 August 2019 No. ZRU 552 "About privatization of the parcels of land of nonagricultural appointment."*

The Law also stipulates which land plots cannot be privatized: (i) land plots located in territories that do not have approved and published layout plans; (ii) land plots with mineral deposits, strategic state property that cannot be subject to privatization; (iii) land plots that are part of the lands designated for environmental, recreational, and historical-cultural purposes, as well as lands of forest and water funds and public lands of cities and towns (e.g., squares, streets, roads, boulevards); (iv) land plots infected with hazardous substances and susceptible to biogenic contamination; and (v) land plots provided to residents of free economic and small industrial zone. However, on several occasions, contractors have raised buildings in public areas based on approvals obtained some years ago or, in some cases, municipal-approved applications for "temporary" commercial use of public spaces—which have become a topic for public debate on the use of public space. Civil society has also played an active role in voicing views on this matter. Legal entities and citizens claiming resident rights may apply for the right of privatizing properties they currently occupy to the designated Commission. If the application is approved, the payment takes place and the transaction is to be ratified by the Municipality and recorded by the Cadaster Agency. The privatization of free land plots is to take place via online auction. Legal entities and citizens may apply for the development of businesses and for the construction of residential properties. Further details on the application of the Law were left to subsequent regulations to be published in September 2019, which have not yet been issued to date.

On 13 August 2019, the government also issued the Presidential Decree "on additional measures to enhance protection of private property and guarantees of ownership rights," to "fundamentally improve organization of works in support of entrepreneurial initiatives as well as expand access of entrepreneurs to financial resources and production infrastructure."[72] The Decree stipulates that in order to test its regulations and procedures, non-agricultural land privatization will be piloted in the Syrdarya Region before it is applied nationwide. This pilot program, currently limited to individuals, is currently implemented and is expected to continue until March 2021. Legal entities will likely be able to apply for land privatization after this date, according to the current forecast.

Urban Neighborhoods Upgrading Program

In June 2018, a national program, named "Obod Makhalla," or Prosperous Neighborhood, was launched to upgrade the state of urban neighborhoods in the cities of Uzbekistan.[73] A 2-year work program (2018–2019) was issued, listing 220 neighborhoods with a total population of 980,000, in cities big and small, that would benefit from the program. Around 38% of the beneficiary population was located in the neighborhoods of Tashkent. Investments were to be financed via a combination of central government transfers and local government resources, with room for international financing, community and private sector contributions, and bank loans, according to the Decree.

The work program foresaw the construction and repair of urban infrastructure, such as road networks and bus stops; water and sanitation; street lighting; and gas, electrical and heat lines. It also included social infrastructure, such as markets, artisanal production areas, community centers, playgrounds, preschools and schools, health care, and sports facilities. Housing estates would benefit from landscaping and watering systems, repair and maintenance of building roofs, facades, elevators, utility systems, gardens, and waste collection.

---

[72]   CIS Legislation. 2019. *Presidential Decree of the Republic of Uzbekistan of 13 August 2019 No. UP-5780 "About additional measures for strengthening of protection of private property and guarantees of the rights of owners, radical enhancement of system of the organization of works on support of entrepreneurial initiatives, and also expansion of access for subjects of entrepreneurship to financial resources and production infrastructure."*

[73]   O'zsanoatqurilishmateriallari. 2018. *On the issues of approval of the main parameters of the program "Obod makhalla" and ensuring their execution.*

While no reporting is available on the implementation status of the Obod Makhalla program, the integrated neighborhood rehabilitation approach is of interest, and at scale, could replace the traditional single sector investment approach. Public transport systems could be better integrated to allow smoother cross city mobility. This is the only government program specifically targeting the quality of the living conditions and urban environment of Uzbek cities, but has so far received limited financial allocations. The 2018 program budget was only $1.3 million in total, and no figures for 2019 or subsequent years have been made available.

Housing Finance

In May 2019, the government issued Presidential Decree No. 5715 "on additional measures for the development and expansion of the mortgage market," which opens the way for housing finance reform. ADB has followed suit with the preparation and approval of the Mortgage Market Sector Development Program in November 2019, currently under implementation.[74] An ADB sector development program aims to develop a market-based residential mortgage market by (i) designing and implementing a new housing policy, reforming housing subsidies, and reviewing the legal and regulatory framework; (ii) strengthening the institutional framework to administer housing policy and subsidies by establishing a Housing Assistance Unit in the Ministry of Finance; and (iii) making long-term fixed-rate local currency funds available to banks to enable them to expand their range of residential mortgage loan products through the establishment of the Uzbekistan Mortgage Refinancing Company (footnote 74).

The government also recognizes the need to gradually replace or phase out the existing programs and move to a market-based mortgage finance mechanism in addressing the housing needs of the population. Additional regulations were recently adopted:

- Presidential Decree No. 5886 in November 2019 "on additional measures to improve mortgage lending mechanisms."
- Cabinet of Ministers Decree No. 182 in May 2020 "on additional measures to improve housing conditions and further expand the mortgage market."
- Cabinet of Ministers Decree No. 182 in March 2020 "on approval of the regulations on subsidies to citizens for the purchase of houses."
- Resolution of the Cabinet of Ministers No. 576 in September 2020 "on the introduction of a simplified system of mortgage loans for the construction and reconstruction of individual housing."

Reforms and Investments in Urban-Related Sectors

Water supply and sanitation. Measures to reorganize WSS institutions and initiate financial and cost recovery mechanisms are not specifically targeting the urban sector, as reforms and related investments intend to provide better services in both urban and rural areas.

The first phase of the reforms began in January 2016, when the 14 regional "Suvokovas" or water supply companies were created through a merger of urban and rural service providers responsible for both water supply and sewerage services, with assets owned jointly by regional and local governments. The second phase was initiated in April 2017 and focuses on the institutional framework for improved sector policy and governance. Specifically, this phase resulted in the creation of the new Ministry of Housing and Communal Services (MHCS),

---

[74]   ADB. 2019. *Report and Recommendation of the President to the Board of Directors: Proposed Loan to the Republic of Uzbekistan for the Mortgage Market Sector Development Program.* Manila.

the State Water Inspectorate (technical compliance mandate), and the Clean Water Drinking Fund, among others. In parallel, the government has initiated the Program for the Comprehensive Development and Modernization of Water Supply and Sewerage Systems, 2017–2021.[75]

Presidential Decree No. 5883 and Presidential Resolution No. 4536 of 26 November 2019 called for the establishment of a Joint-Stock Company, JSC Uzsuvtaminot, to manage the transition of the national Suvokovas into independent limited liability companies (LLC). The transition from State Unitary Enterprise status to LLC was completed in May 2020. In accordance with Presidential Resolution No. 4536, the Agency for Management of State Assets will be the shareholder of state-owned shares in the JSC Uzsuvtaminot, while 100% of shares of regional LLCs will be owned by JSC Uzsuvtaminot. The roles and responsibilities of sector agencies are further defined in Presidential Resolution No. 6074 (September 2020) "on measures aimed at further development of drinking water supply and sewerage system, as well as relevant investment projects efficiency enhancement," which clarifies JSC as the operator and the MHCS as responsible for policy and strategy.[76] The resolution supports decentralization and gives greater authority to regions in tariff setting following the principle of full cost recovery. While these reforms aim to strengthen accountability, efficiency, and sustainability in the water sector, transforming the newly formed LLCs into successful operating independent business entities will require more time.

The government is considering private sector participation, broadly introduced by the World Bank and the Swiss Economic and Cooperation Agency program in Khorezm region and Fergana valley, which aims to replicate best practices on efficient operation and maintenance and management of local water supply systems. Meanwhile, JSC Uzsuvtaminot aims to digitalize the WSS system, reduce NRW levels, improve operation and maintenance practices, and consider any type of PPP-based approach to improve and expand the delivery and quality of WSS services. ADB is providing support through technical assistance advisory services, assisting MHCS in structuring PPP schemes for cities in Kashkadarya, Navoi, and Namangan regions.

The State Investment Program identified 36 high-priority infrastructure projects to be initiated within a 5-year period. A total of $1.35 billion was assigned to this program, 55% of which was earmarked for funding by IFIs and the remaining funds would come from the government budget. Around 45% of the total investments over this period is planned for improving living conditions and supporting economic development (footnote 75). Similarly, Presidential Resolution No. 4040, issued on 30 November 2018, established the development and implementation of new tariff procedures to allow sustainable cost recovery in the sector, to be supported by a national water metering program. Presidential Decree No. 6074 included a new tariff policy based on the principle of full cost recovery.

The National Water Supply and Wastewater System Development and Modernization Plan (2009–2020) was set to address wastewater treatment. The government also has a State Program for the Development of Aral Sea Region for 2017–2021, which includes expanding water supply for all the cities in Karakalpakstan.[77] The rehabilitation of the Tuyamuyun water treatment plant and the construction of a new plant in Mangit (Amudarya district) are also part of ADB's projects.

Solid waste management. The government is reforming the sector by (i) enacting an SWM strategy and related government resolutions; (ii) creating SWM service zones in urban areas, to be implemented through PPPs;

---

[75]   World Bank. 2020. *Project Appraisal Document: Water Services and Institutional Support Project.*
[76]   Government of Uzbekistan. 2020. *Presidential Decree 6074 on measures aimed at further development of drinking water supply and sewerage system, as well as relevant investment projects efficiency enhancement.* Tashkent.
[77]   Communal Services Agency of the Republic of Uzbekistan. 2017. *Initial Environmental Examination: Western Uzbekistan Water Supply System Development Project* (prepared for ADB).

(iii) establishing "Toza Hudud" under the State Committee for Environmental Protection (SCEEP), an SWM state unitary enterprise to provide small urban centers, peri-urban and rural SWM services; (iv) mobilizing recyclers; (v) introducing best-practice SWM technologies; and (vi) incentivizing foreign direct investment.

ADB has assisted Uzbekistan in rehabilitating and expanding the SWM system in Tashkent and in formulating the national SWM strategy. Initiatives like the SWM project in Samarkand City implemented by the Agence Française de Développement also complement ADB support in assisting the government to realize the national SWM strategy (footnote 38).

With regard to SWM improvements in small urban centers, peri-urban and rural areas, the government is now implementing three broad phases of sector reforms to (i) strengthen the regulatory framework, rationalize and operationalize SWM service delivery institutions, address acute municipal solid waste collection deficiencies, and improve dumpsites; (ii) achieve universal SWM collection coverage, and transit from existing dumpsites to modern sanitary landfills; and (iii) accelerate waste reduction and recycling initiatives, and incorporate alternative technologies. The government has already established the "Toza Hudud," has transferred municipality assets to them, and has begun to improve small urban centers, peri-urban and rural collection systems, and dumpsites (footnote 38).

District heating. In 2017, the government transferred the district heating services to the MHCS and approved the Program on the Development of District Heating System for 2018–2022. This program aims to address fractured policy frameworks, and modernize and upgrade district heating service infrastructure with new energy-efficient technologies. In order to do so, the program prioritizes the establishment of automated metering systems, and the replacement of antiquated heat-boiler equipment, distribution networks, and in-house heating systems. Transitioning from open heat systems to closed ones with the installation of building-level individual heat substations (IHS) is necessary in decentralizing district heating services and making them cost-effective (footnote 39).

A World Bank District Heating Energy Efficiency Project, which was approved in 2018, aims to address the inefficiencies of the current system by introducing a new design concept of an energy-efficient closed heat system that meets the heating needs of the population in Andijan, Bukhara, Chirchik, Samarkand, and the Sergeli District of Tashkent City. These five pilot cities will serve as replicable models of modernization that catalyzes private financing (footnote 39). However, energy efficiency standards in the housing and commercial construction sectors is an important reform and requires a stronger enforcement mechanism under the Ministry of Construction, Ministry of Energy, Uzstandard, and MHCS.

Electricity and gas. The Cabinet of Ministers Resolution No. 310 dated 13 April 2019 adopted a new electricity tariff methodology that increases the financial viability of the sector by progressively adjusting tariffs to full cost recovery levels while improving environmental sustainability and resilience to climate change. A tariff council was established under President Resolution No. 3981 dated 23 October 2018 to regulate the tariff setting (footnote 40). In addition, the creation of the Ministry of Energy in January 2019 responds to a greater effort of energy sector reform as stated by Uzbekistan's 2018 strategy. Similarly, the government decided to split Uzbekenergo, the state energy company, into three entities to separate production, transportation, and distribution of electricity. Moreover, the identification of new greenfield projects that foster renewable energy projects and PPPs for the rehabilitation of existing infrastructure is underway.

The government is rolling out advanced electricity metering infrastructure nationwide with target completion by 2022 to reduce energy system losses, increase energy efficiency, and improve transparency and accountability in the sector. The alignment of tariffs to true costs will also significantly contribute to the government's wider campaign of improving energy efficiency and loss reduction, which in turn could have significant climate mitigation co-benefits in addition to adaptation co-benefits through increased reliability (footnote 40). Additionally, Uzbekneftegas has undergone a reform process to promote financial transparency and assets modernization. These measures are being supported by ADB along with the adoption of International Financial Reporting Standards and the sale of Uzbekneftegas' vast portfolio of non-core assets (footnote 40).

Presidential Decree No. 4512 of 2013 "on the measures for further development of alternative energy sources" provides for the production of photovoltaic panels in Navoi, a first step into the current national policy regarding solar power. As part of its Intended Nationally Determined Contribution (INDC) under the United Nations Framework Convention on Climate Change (UNFCCC), Uzbekistan in 2017 committed to bring up the share of solar energy in the total energy balance of the country to 6% by 2030.[78] In May 2020, the government approved a concept note for ensuring electricity supply in Uzbekistan for 2020–2030. This document lays out the medium-term and long-term goals for the growing energy sector, such as modernizing and reconstructing the existing power plants (mostly thermal power plants), building new power plants, improving the electrical metering systems and tariff policies, and developing renewable energy sources.[79] The European Bank for Reconstruction and Development is also supporting the Ministry of Energy to achieve carbon neutrality by 2050 through developing renewable power plants, modernizing the electricity grid, and decommissioning older thermal power plants. ADB and the World Bank are also supporting the solar energy projects.

Environmental protection. The European Investment Bank approved a loan of more than $100 million to mitigate the impact of the Aral Sea disappearance and improve the environmental and socioeconomic conditions in the area.[80] To address health risks, adaptation measures in the Tashkent and Syrdarya regions are also being taken as part of a pilot WHO project. Health-care facilities are being equipped with a data collection system that receives meteorological and health data to raise early warnings on climate-sensitive health risks. The project is supported by the Ministry of Health and by UzHydromet. Some positive remedial actions in pollution management have been lately carried out by the SCEEP, like shutting down operations in a cement factory that had failed to meet standards of dust collection in the Andijan region.[81] Similarly, SCEEP plans to increase the pollution monitoring capacity around industrial plants, and set up static monitoring stations within and near plant sites.[82]

External Assistance

ADB's Lending and Technical Assistance Program

ADB has been Uzbekistan's leading international development partner, supporting its financial and technical requirements since 1995 in three strategic areas: private sector development, reduction of economic and social disparities, and regional cooperation and integration. ADB has committed loans, grants, and technical assistance amounting to $10.1 billion for Uzbekistan (Table 4). In 2020, ADB committed six projects and programs, and one grant totaling $1.1 billion. To combat COVID-19, ADB funding supported the procurement of medical supplies and equipment, prepared additional hospitals and laboratories, supported businesses and minimized job losses, and expanded social protection.

---

[78] United Nations Framework Convention on Climate Change. 2018. *Intended Nationally Determined Contributions of the Republic of Uzbekistan*.
[79] *Energy Central*. 2020. Uzbekistan Adopted the Concept of Supplying the Country with Electric Energy for 2020–2030. 4 May.
[80] *European Investment Bank* (EIB). 2019. EIB and Uzbekistan Take First Steps towards a EUR100 Million Investment Program for the Recovery of the Aral Sea. 24 September.
[81] *Global Cement*. 2020. State Committee on Ecology and Environmental Protection Suspends Cement Production at Sing Lida Plant. 26 February.
[82] *Global Cement*. 2020. Uzbekistan Starts Pollution Monitoring. 22 January.

The water and other urban infrastructure and services sector has benefited from about $850 million of financing, mostly in the water and sanitation and SWM subsectors. Related projects are all contributing to the provision of urban infrastructure and to the reform of relevant institutions and service delivery mechanisms, as described in Sections I.6 and II.2.

Table 4: ADB Cumulative Lending, Grant and Technical Assistance Commitments, end of 2020

Uzbekistan: Cumulative Loans, Grants, Equity Investments, Technical Assistance and Trade Finance, Supply Chain Finance and Microfinance Program Commitments[a,b,c,d]

Sector	No.	Total Amount ($ million)[e]	% of Total Amount[e]	COVID-19 Response ($ million)[e]
Projects and Technical Assistance	236	10,113.38	93.73	607.32
Agriculture, Natural Resources, and Rural Development	33	784.95	7.27	–
Education	23	298.03	2.76	–
Energy	37	2,494.85	23.12	–
Finance	40	1,942.37	18.00	0.47
Health	9	193.96	1.80	105.36
Industry and Trade	4	176.83	1.64	0.21
Information and Communication Technology	–	0.18	0.00	0.07
Multisector	–	0.28	0.00	–
Public Sector Management	23	1,134.55	10.51	501.10
Transport	37	2,053.53	19.03	–
Water and Other Urban Infrastructure and Services	30	1,033.85	9.58	0.11
Trade and Supply Chain Finance and Microfinance[f]	619	676.97	6.27	126.87
Finance	312	338.48	3.14	63.43
Industry and Trade	307	338.48	3.14	63.43
Total	**855**	**10,790.00**	**1.00**	**734.00**

– = nil, ADB = Asian Development Bank, COVID-19 = coronavirus disease, DMC = developing member country, TA = technical assistance.

a Grants and technical assistance include ADB-administered cofinancing.

b Includes sovereign and nonsovereign loans and technical assistance.

c Using primary sector in reporting of commitments.

d Financing for TA projects with regional coverage is distributed to their specific DMCs where breakdown is available.

e Numbers may not sum precisely because of rounding.

f ADB-financed commitments from nonsovereign revolving programs of which $597.29 million is short-term.

Source: ADB. 2021. Asian Development and Uzbekistan: Fact Sheet.

Among the active projects in the portfolio, the finance sector policy lending operation, Mortgage Market Sector Development Program, is directly related to the urban sector. Approved in 2019 for $200 million, the program aims to strengthen the capacity of the banking sector in providing mortgages to support residential housing development, which is a critical component for achieving greater and more equitable urbanization and livable cities.

The current ADB country partnership strategy (CPS) 2019–2023 promotes progress in supporting private sector development, reducing economic and social disparities, and promoting regional cooperation and integration.[83] As part of the outcomes that ADB intends to contribute to, the CPS highlights the themes of urbanization and improved urban development practices:

- integrated urban planning and management for selected cities and towns,
- upgrades of rural and urban service infrastructure,
- improvement of access to infrastructure and social services through PPPs, and
- mitigation of infrastructure constraints to private sector development.

The country operations business plan 2021–2023 targets the design and approval of urban operations totalling $663 million in ADB finance with technical assistance of $3.8 million to support (i) integrated urban development; (ii) drinking water and sanitation system improvement; (iii) solid waste collection and waste disposal; and (iv) policy reforms, institutional development, and capacity building.

In 2019, ADB approved the preparation of the Integrated Urban Development Project, which will focus on the four cities of Djizzak, Khiva, Havast, and Yangiyer. The project is slated for approval in 2022 for a loan value of $100 million. This will be the first ADB engagement in support of the government's reforms and investments in urban development. The project will provide inclusive and resilient urban services in these four cities that are experiencing stagnant growth, which has been exacerbated by the COVID-19 pandemic. It will demonstrate integrated, strategic, and local development, and strengthen urban governance and institutional capacity as an effective approach for building back better. Physical investments will include a mix of water supply, sanitation, SWM, urban public spaces, and tourism infrastructure and services, combined with capacity building to strengthen urban governance and management.

ADB Strategy 2030 and the GrEEEn Cities Approach

In July 2018, ADB published its Strategy 2030, Achieving a Prosperous, Inclusive, Resilient and Sustainable Asia and the Pacific. The strategy states that in lower middle-income countries, such as Uzbekistan, ADB will promote green and inclusive infrastructure, social services and social protection, sustainable urbanization, and overall structural changes to enhance productivity and competitiveness through public sector reforms, private sector investment, and domestic resource mobilization. ADB will also support the reform of state-owned enterprises (SOEs) and increase private sector operations by attracting private investors and bringing in commercial co-financiers.[84]

One of ADB Strategy 2030's seven key operational priorities is making cities more livable (priority 4), which reiterates ADB's commitment to build green, competitive, and inclusive cities through crosscutting projects that promote urban health, urban mobility, gender equality, and environmental sustainability. Moreover, it highlights the importance of considering climate resilience and disaster risk management during integrated urban planning,

83 ADB. *Uzbekistan: Country Partnership Strategy 2019–2023*. Manila.
84 ADB. 2018. *Strategy 2030: Achieving a Prosperous, Inclusive, Resilient and Sustainable Asia and the Pacific*. Manila.

particularly in countries like Uzbekistan, where hilly and mountainous geographic features aggravate climate change effects (footnote 84).

Another relevant reference is ADB's GrEEEn Cities approach, whereby urban development and environmental planning are integrated in the pursuit of three key urban dimensions: (i) economic competitiveness, (ii) environmental quality, and (iii) equity (the three "E"s).[85] Economic competitiveness encompasses service delivery efficiency, infrastructures asset management, operation and maintenance, financial innovation, PPPs, revenue generation, and entrepreneurship and job creation. Environmental quality covers natural resource efficiency, low-carbon technology, climate resilience, and disaster risk management. Equity comprises inclusiveness, accessibility, affordability, and resiliency considerations.

According to this conceptual model, "enablers" play a critical role in integrating urban development and environmental planning and in achieving a successful and livable city. These enablers are policies, strategies, sector plans, regulations, finance, governance, institutions, civil society, and the private sector. Consensus building, visioning, and stakeholder ownership can be achieved through preparing GrEEEn city action plans, which include investment programs and financing mechanisms, as well as establishing urban management partnerships that will provide peer-to-peer learning, decision-support systems, and skills training.

These ADB references, at the corporate and sector levels, provide guidance for identifying possible areas of engagement with the Government of Uzbekistan in its pursuit of urbanization and higher-quality urban development for the benefit of its economy and citizens. These opportunities are further explored in Part IV of this report.

Other Development Partners

International finance institutions and development agencies have been supporting the Government of Uzbekistan in urban development and urban infrastructure and services sector. To date, a total of $2.8 billion in loans and grants have been provided by ADB, the World Bank, European Bank for Reconstruction and Development, European Investment Bank, Islamic Development Bank, Asian Infrastructure Investment Bank, Agence Française de Développement, OPEC Fund for International Development, and Japan International Cooperation Agency. All these development partners, including ADB and United Nations agencies, have also provided research and technical assistance in a variety of related fields.

Appendix 5 presents a full list of active projects and projects that have been approved or under preparation. Majority of the urban infrastructure projects supported by development partners are in the WSS sector, followed by SWM and energy, including rehabilitation of power stations and substations, electrical metering, and street lighting. Urban-relevant operations include support to the cadaster agency and institutional support to the ongoing infrastructure sector reforms.

The World Bank's Medium-Size Cities Integrated Urban Development Project, approved in 2018 and under implementation, is the only operation with a direct urban development focus. The project provided a loan of $100 million to support the cities of Kagan, Chortok, and Yangiyul in improving urban services and enhancing public urban spaces. It finances a targeted bundle of integrated and multisector investments to contribute to the enhancement of selected public urban spaces and to improve livability. It also provides institutional strengthening and capacity building of the staff of cities and local government agencies, tailored to their specific needs. Local government staff have been trained on asset management systems, management of integrated urban mobility,

---

[85] ADB. 2014. *Enabling GrEEEn Cities: An Operational Framework for Integrated Urban Development in Southeast Asia.* Manila.

sustainable tourism development, and cooperation with the private sector. The project also supports the preparation of the national medium-size cities program (NMSCP), which could be scaled up in the near future.

Another World Bank contribution to the understanding of the urban sector is its Urban Policy Note of 2017, developed as part of preparing the Medium-Size Cities Integrated Urban Development Project. The Note highlights the positive links between urbanization and economic growth, and opportunities to accelerate the process, to the benefit of agglomeration economics. It also highlights the risks of accelerated urbanization in the absence of robust property rights and in the context of outdated urban planning approaches. Such accelerated urbanization could be the consequence of liberalizing land property and removing mobility constraints, which could trigger land speculation.

III. Challenges for Sustainable Urbanization to 2030

Directing Future Urbanization

The Action Strategy attached to the Decree "on the strategy for the further development of the Republic of Uzbekistan" of February 2017 articulates "integrated and balanced socio-economic development of regions, districts and cities, [and] the optimal and efficient use of their potential" as one of the national priorities. Three years later, Uzbekistan still needs a territorial strategy in regional development to harness the potential of urbanization as a driving force of economic growth, to capture the related urban agglomeration benefits and direct urban development accordingly.

The country is bound to reach a 49.4% rate of urbanization by 2030. This rate is well below the government's goal of 60%, if it just maintains the regional compounded annual growth rate (CAGR) of urbanization during 2010–2019, as shown in Appendix 1. The region of Tashkent (including the capital city) and the regions of the Fergana Valley (including the cities of Andijan, Namangan, and Fergana) would have 11.2 million urban residents by 2030, against the 9.4 million of 2019. Except for Namangan, these regions and cities would have lower levels of urbanization by 2030 compared to that of 2019. Only the Syrdarya region would see a likely increase in its urbanization rate. While the lifting of the *propiska* requirements may increase annual urban growth rates, particularly in the Tashkent metropolitan region, further investments in making cities more attractive for businesses and citizens alike will be needed to encourage an increase in rural-to-urban migration.

Directing future urbanization toward a more balanced regional growth and the reinforcement of some secondary cities is crucial, otherwise, Tashkent's role as the country's dominant urban area would become overwhelming. Also, the socioeconomic divide between the four easternmost regions (Tashkent region and the Fergana Valley) and the rest of the national territory would further increase, risking social tensions and national cohesion and undermining economic growth potential.

However, rather than constraining the urbanization of the Tashkent region and the Fergana Valley, the government could seek ways to strategically plan and reinforce the role of secondary urban areas— primarily the key cities such as Samarkand, Bukhara, and Karshi, and the smaller cities such as Urgench and Nukus in the northwest, as well as Djizzak and Gulistan located between Tashkent and Samarkand. This would move Uzbekistan toward a polycentric development and support regional development, enhancing opportunities for growth and welfare (Part IV.1).

Supporting Municipal Development

Promoting greater and more equitable urbanization would also require strengthening the role of municipalities in urban development. Municipal governments currently has no administrative autonomy and responds to regional governors just like district administrations do. The only exceptions are the capital city, which has the equivalent status of a region; the cities of the Republic of Karakalpakstan; and the cities with special status of "republican subordination," which benefit from direct reporting to the central authorities and from relevant administrative privileges. The legal setup of these cities could be reviewed to see whether the administrative model put in place for republican subordination can guide further decentralization.

Further decentralization would also support more equitable urbanization in the next decade. The World Bank recommends three steps in the decentralization process: (i) review and clarify the assignments of functions across government levels, (ii) improve transparency and predictability of fiscal transfers through a rule-based system, and (iii) consider providing greater revenue autonomy for SNGs (footnote 31).

However, greater decentralization and strengthening the role of municipalities in urban development will also require improving their technical, organizational, and financial management capacities. Accelerating decentralization is an area of reform that would play an important role in supporting equitable urbanization, as cities become the focus of economic development and as they become more complex entities requiring more advanced management systems. In addition to capacities, the methodologies, approaches, and instruments to be used by local authorities should be considered. Another issue is the availability and reliability of data, as addressed in the Decree by the President on Statistics of 3 August 2020. If no instruments and methodology are made available, increased capacities will not be able to transform planning and decision making from short term to long term, given the available resources and the goals to be achieved.

According to the World Bank, the current system of intergovernmental finance arrangements is highly discretionary and creates uncertainty for a SNG (footnote 31). This is caused by the variation of taxes shared and ad hoc budgetary transfers that interfere with predictability of incoming yearly resources. Public financial management would benefit from a rule-based, transparent transfer system (such as in Indonesia) that fosters efficiency and prevents political manipulation or abrupt disruptions to the income that SNG expect to receive. Furthermore, the link between expenditure and revenue resources needs to be restored to promote efficiency in SNGs. Such directions can provide guidance for the next reforms in this area.

The creation of an urban land market via land privatization program, the influx of workforce into the cities following the end of the *propiska* system, and an increase in urban housing supply and associated urban infrastructure and services are big challenges for municipal governments, which would have to support and facilitate such processes. However, they also represent opportunities of leveraging greater tax resources for municipalities, provided the fiscal system would allow them to do so. It is safe to assume that with land privatization, the establishment of a land market, and the expansion of residential construction activities, municipalities would see significant increases in their revenues from property taxation. As citizens become wealthier, municipalities can also eventually increase property tax rates, thereby raising more resources for the provision of urban services.

Reforming Urban Planning

European style urban planning (e.g., defined city center; wide, radial tree-lined streets; public monuments) was introduced in Uzbekistan at the time of Russian colonization in the mid-19th century, starting with Tashkent. This was established as the Russian capital, initially adjacent to the existing Uzbek settlement, and laid out according to European urban planning principles. Over the course of a century, the city would become the de facto capital of Soviet Central Asia, and the fourth-largest city in the Soviet Union. Its urban planning and development were the result of concerted efforts in modernizing the region and introducing advanced urban systems, aimed at rallying the support of the local population for a secular, egalitarian, and controlled way of life.[86] The same urban planning principles were applied to secondary cities, before and after independence.

Soviet planning is still apparent today in its legacy of wide avenues, monumental vistas, expansive but hardly pedestrian-friendly public spaces, and segregated urban functions. Uzbek cities have a very low density, which is currently only 34 persons per hectare in the case of Tashkent.[87] In this case, the network of main broad avenues has been laid over a pattern of traditional, self-enclosed neighborhoods or mahallas mostly consisting of single-family homes, one- or two-story high, a legacy of traditional Asian urban layouts, with scarce secondary and tertiary road networks. Urban planners have simply superimposed the location and construction of housing estates, which were mostly erected during the Soviet Union era, with no real integration of the formal and informal city fabrics.

As individual motorization rapidly takes over public transportation, the limits of a low-density urban form and the insufficient internal road network are becoming apparent, and congestion is already manifesting itself and starting to erode Tashkent's efficiency. Urban planning would have to be integrated with land-use and transport planning to move the city toward a future of greater density and compact urban form, and of renewed urban transport systems.

Tashkent has been expanding outward and incorporating further rural areas in its municipal boundaries. The recent construction of the outer ring-road and various trunk roads, tunnels, and bridges has facilitated access to more remote sites, and new housing estates have been lately constructed south of the Chirchiq River. State land ownership and the absence of a land market have facilitated such low-density growth. Similar patterns of growth are observed in secondary cities.

A new generation of urban master plans is needed to translate a national urbanization strategy into specific growth strategies for Uzbekistan's capital and for its secondary cities. Such plans would have the goals of facilitating sustainable urbanization through urban competitiveness; equitable urban redevelopment; better access to urban services; and improvements in public health, environmental quality, and resilience to natural hazards and climate change risks. Most importantly, the plans should focus on integrated urban development, bringing together the multiple components of a city and its suburbs including economic, environmental, and cultural dimensions with infrastructure linkages in favor of urban livability—as opposed to planning separately the various infrastructure systems and investments as was done in the past. This requires a holistic perspective and integrated approach. These goals can only be achieved with stronger urban governance and institutional capacity to plan, finance, and respond to citizen and business needs in an efficient and accountable manner. One promising recent reform is Presidential Decree UP-6119 "on approval of the strategy of modernization, accelerated and innovative development of the construction industry of the Republic of Uzbekistan for 2021–2025" of November 2020. The decree calls for modernizing the urban planning process. It also requires the Ministry of Construction to prepare master plans for all 119 cities and 25% of the 1,071 urban settlements by 2025, and calls for greater citizen participation in the planning process.

---

86   P. Stronski. 2010. *Tashkent: Forging a Soviet City, 1930–1966*. Pittsburgh: University of Pittsburgh Press.
87   Comparator regional cities present higher densities: Almaty (40), Bishkek (50), Astana (51), and Dushanbe (55). Larger cities in the Middle East have significantly higher densities: Tehran (80), Istanbul (110). Demographia. 2021. *Demographia World Urban Areas*. 17th edition. June.

Enabling Territorial Mobility

A key goal of Presidential Decree "on measures to fundamentally improve the process of urbanization" of January 2019 is freeing citizens from the constraints of residency permits (*propiska* system), and enable people to freely move from rural to urban areas. Earlier, residency permits were required nationwide to access basic socioeconomic rights (i.e., apply for identification papers; access employment; obtain pension payments and other social benefits such as health care, education, housing, and rights to open a business; get married and register children; and vote). Permanent residency permits are issued by authorities based on restrictive conditions of formal employment, particularly in Tashkent and the Tashkent region.

At the time of *propiska* (lifted for Tashkent city in September 2020), estimates of temporary or illegal residents present in Tashkent varied from the official numbers of about 320,000 to higher unofficial estimates of over 1 million. This problem affected secondary cities as well. Samarkand is officially estimated to host more than 250,000 temporary or illegal residents (footnote 5), which would already surpass the population count of the city by 50%, but many more could be present. The inadvertent violators of the registration procedure were typically the most vulnerable, low-income groups, such as migrants from rural areas, refugees, internally displaced persons, young families, orphanage graduates, former inmates, large families, people with disabilities, and homeless people. Buying a house in the city for those groups is an impossible task, and the lack of registration did not allow them to get an affordable housing nor arrange a mortgage (footnote 5).

The Presidential Decree No. 5984 of 22 April 2020 led to the relaxation of the residency permit system for Tashkent and the Tashkent region, allowing citizens to obtain official residence provided they purchase a housing unit from a primary or secondary market. This provision follows the 2017 Decree that granted residence rights for buyers of newly constructed apartments and housing units in Tashkent and the Tashkent region. In both cases, these policy provisions are linked to the rise of new residential buildings in the capital city in recent years. In September 2020, significant changes were introduced under Presidential Decree No. 5984 on the *propiska* system, allowing every citizen to obtain temporary or permanent registration, eliminating the term *propiska*, and lifting the need for a registration stamp in a citizen's passport.

Increasing Urban Housing and Infrastructure Supply

The issue of affordability of real estate in Tashkent for the majority of its population is a significant challenge, and being addressed by the government through *propiska* reforms. Currently, more than 72% of households residing in the city could not afford to live in their housing if they do not own the house. That is to say, renting their current housing at market value would be impossible for them despite enjoying the highest average incomes in the country. At the extreme, renting in Tashkent city was measured at 14.8 times higher than annual household consumption in 2018, and 10.8 times higher than annual household income. Per the home value-based measure, the city of Tashkent is more unaffordable than many famous, exclusive metropolitan areas, such as San Francisco in the United States and Vancouver in Canada (footnote 5).

The relaxation of *propiska* requirements for buyers of housing units, particularly in Tashkent, may only affect a small segment of the current urban population, attracting wealthier Uzbeks from other regions to acquire property and move to Tashkent, further accelerating the growth of the capital city to the detriment of secondary ones.

Assuming territorial mobility will be achieved, pursuing the agglomeration benefits of improved transport corridors and hubs, trade and border facilitation, free economic zones, and related job creation will cause a significant shift of labor from the rural to the urban areas. This, in turn, will require a major increase in housing supply to face such influx. The current yearly production of about 90,000 units is already insufficient to meet the yearly demand, estimated at about 145,000 units, given new household formation and the accumulated backlog. This demand would only increase on account of the additional internal migration to cities.

Scaling up urbanization and urban development would also require a significant increase in the provision of urban infrastructure and services that are needed to complement the supply of housing. WSS systems, urban roads, drainage systems, public spaces, SWM, district heating, energy and gas distribution, and public transport systems would have to be upgraded.

All these sectors require major financial investments, in addition to robust regulatory frameworks and capable sector institutions. Improving the urban infrastructure and services also require financial mechanisms for cost recovery, pricing structures reflecting the real capital value of assets, operation and maintenance, and service delivery costs that are affordable for the poorer segments of the population. If such reforms were to be implemented, they would also open the way for PPPs in urban infrastructure provision and urban services delivery.

Addressing Environmental Degradation and Climate Change

For Uzbekistan's urbanization to become sustainable, its strategy would have to address the environmental and climate change constraints that the country faces, and that will only become starker in the future. A clear understanding of how such challenges will affect the country's cities would also avoid locking into a pattern of urban development that is dependent on high consumption of water and energy. Uzbekistan's energy waste, water use, and carbon dioxide emissions per unit of GDP are among the highest globally.[88] Improving urban environmental quality and public health would be recognized as an important goal for inclusive and sustainable urbanization. As natural hazards and climate change pose greater risks to Uzbek cities, these can be better mitigated via anticipatory urban planning.

Uzbek cities will experience potentially damaging and life-threatening urban floods at least once in the next 10 years. Hence, project planning decisions, project design, and construction methods must take into account the level of urban flood hazard.[89] Urban resiliency must increase local capacity to manage seismic and climate-related risks by improving early warning systems and the collection of hazard information. Readily available and easy-to-access weather forecasting services and public infrastructure are needed to address earthquake emergencies and climate change impacts.

Uzbekistan has more than 300 sunny days a year, and approximately 75% of the country is desertic. Solar radiation of 176.8 million tonnes of oil equivalent (Mtoe) is found to be technically exploitable, although is not currently commercially available.[90] According to the MIFT Investment Promotion Agency, the gross potential of solar energy in Uzbekistan is estimated at 50,973 Mtoe, which is 99.7% of the total gross potential of all renewable energy sources investigated to date in the country; the technical potential is 176.8 Mtoe (98.6% of the total technical potential of renewable energy).[91] In 2017, as part of its INDC under the UNFCCC, Uzbekistan

88   L. Burunciuc et al. 2018. How Uzbekistan is Transforming into an Open Economy. *Brookings.* 20 December.
89   GFDRR. 2020. Uzbekistan. Urban Flood (accessed 24 June 2020).
90   Japan International Cooperation Agency. 2016. Preparatory Survey (F/S) for Tashkent Thermal Power Cogeneration Plant Construction Project and Master Plan Study in the Republic of Uzbekistan.
91   Government of Uzbekistan, Ministry of Investments and Foreign Trade, Investment Promotion Agency. Fuel Energy Complex.

made a commitment to bring up the share of solar energy in the total energy balance of the country to 6% by 2030 (footnote 79).

Residential renewable energy installations in the form of solar photovoltaic systems and water heaters represent an opportunity for the country, as stated by the Concept Note for Ensuring Electricity Supply in Uzbekistan in 2020–2030.[92] The World Bank's Energy Sector Management Assistance Program funded a least-cost assessment of Uzbekistan's heating sector. The main findings of the assessment point to efficiency and quality of heating and hot water services in cities like Andijan, Bukhara, Chirchik, Samarkand, and Tashkent. The livability of cities, especially during winter months, heavily rely on district heating efficiency, which clearly needs to be upgraded.[93]

The government has revised the building standards for energy-efficient urban and rural housing while promoting small-scale biogas, hydropower, large-scale solar power, and solar water heating. These normative premises could be followed up by investment programs to expand and eventually mainstream the use of renewable energy systems in urban areas to supplement the centralized provision of urban services, such as energy and district heating.

As part of its INDC, Uzbekistan established a carbon intensity target, pledging to decrease emissions of greenhouse gas (GHG) per unit of GDP by 10% by 2030 from its 2010 levels. GHG emissions from vehicles in Tashkent rounded 1.2 metric tons of carbon dioxide equivalent ($MtCO_2$) in 2019 and are expected to double by 2030. The introduction of electric vehicles for passenger cars and commercial vehicles like taxis, buses, and urban delivery trucks aims to tackle this issue. Electrifying urban buses and establishing charging infrastructure would support sustainable transport initiatives and could benefit from financial structuring and incentives.

---

[92]   Government of Uzbekistan, Ministry of Energy. 2020. Concept Note for Ensuring Electricity Supply in Uzbekistan in 2020–2030.
[93]   *Energy Sector Management Assistance Program.* 2018. Uzbekistan: Keeping Urban Dwellers Warm. 12 July.

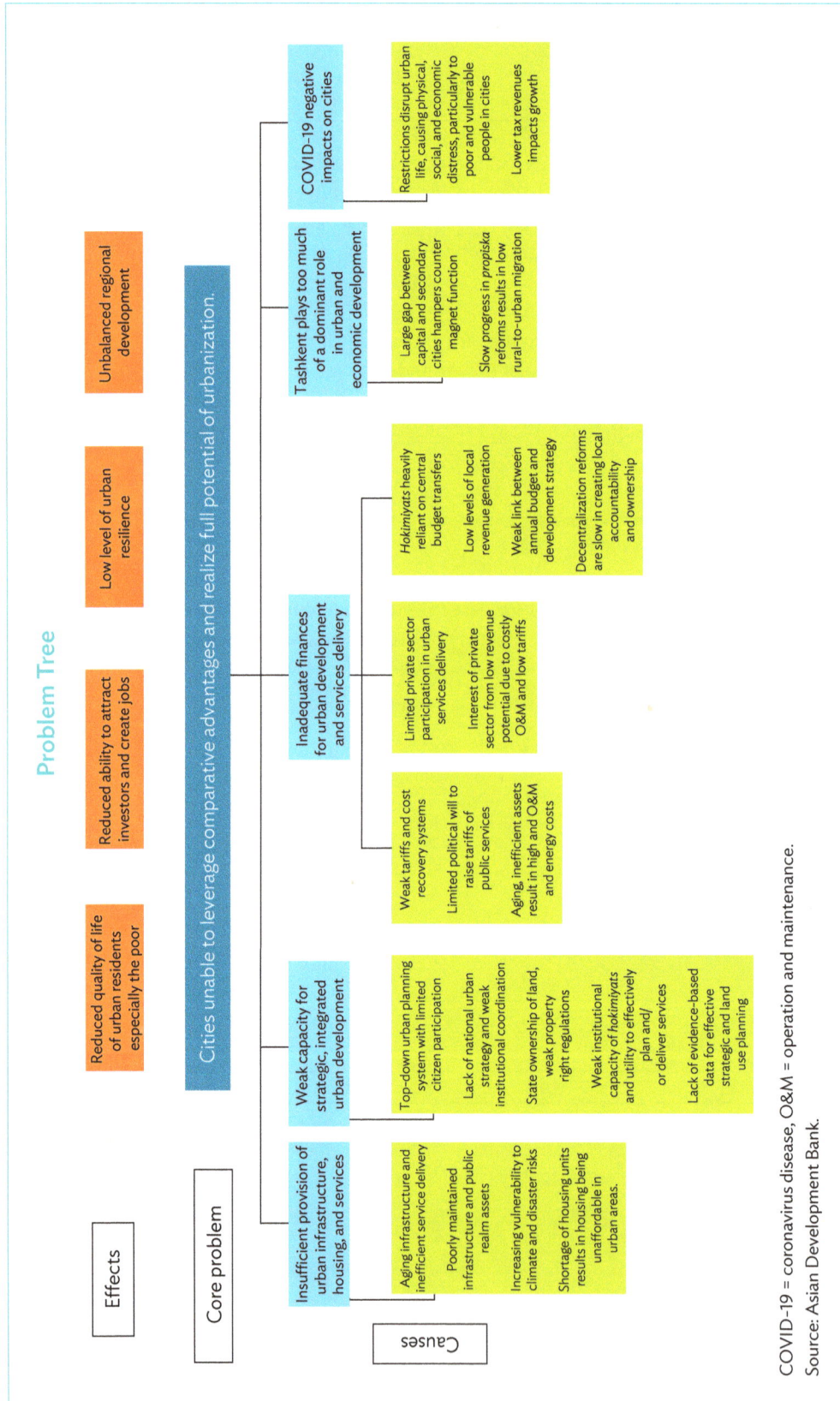

Problem Tree

Effects

| Reduced quality of life of urban residents especially the poor | Reduced ability to attract investors and create jobs | Low level of urban resilience | Unbalanced regional development |

Core problem

Cities unable to leverage comparative advantages and realize full potential of urbanization.

Causes

Insufficient provision of urban infrastructure, housing, and services
- Aging infrastructure and inefficient service delivery
- Poorly maintained infrastructure and public realm assets
- Increasing vulnerability to climate and disaster risks
- Shortage of housing units results in housing being unaffordable in urban areas.

Weak capacity for strategic, integrated urban development
- Top-down urban planning system with limited citizen participation
- Lack of national urban strategy and weak institutional coordination
- State ownership of land, weak property right regulations
- Weak institutional capacity of hokimiyats and utility to effectively plan and/or deliver services
- Lack of evidence-based data for effective strategic and land use planning

Inadequate finances for urban development and services delivery
- Weak tariffs and cost recovery systems
- Limited political will to raise tariffs of public services
- Aging, inefficient assets result in high and O&M and energy costs
- Limited private sector participation in urban services delivery
- Interest of private sector from low revenue potential due to costly O&M and low tariffs
- Hokimiyats heavily reliant on central budget transfers
- Low levels of local revenue generation
- Weak link between annual budget and development strategy
- Decentralization reforms are slow in creating local accountability and ownership

Tashkent plays too much of a dominant role in urban and economic development
- Large gap between capital and secondary cities hampers counter magnet function
- Slow progress in propiska reforms results in low rural-to-urban migration

COVID-19 negative impacts on cities
- Restrictions disrupt urban life, causing physical, social, and economic distress, particularly to poor and vulnerable people in cities
- Lower tax revenues impacts growth

COVID-19 = coronavirus disease, O&M = operation and maintenance.
Source: Asian Development Bank.

IV.   Making Uzbek Cities More Livable

Competitive Cities

Capturing Agglomeration Benefits

The main transport corridors being built under the CAREC program and the Belt and Road Initiative could become positive drivers for future urbanization, and help Uzbekistan capture the agglomeration benefits of further urbanization, if complementary public policies are put in place to reap the related benefits for the cities that are affected (Map 1). Key transport corridors in the country are illustrated in Appendix 2.

Map 1: Welfare Gains from Transport Investments and Border Cost Reductions

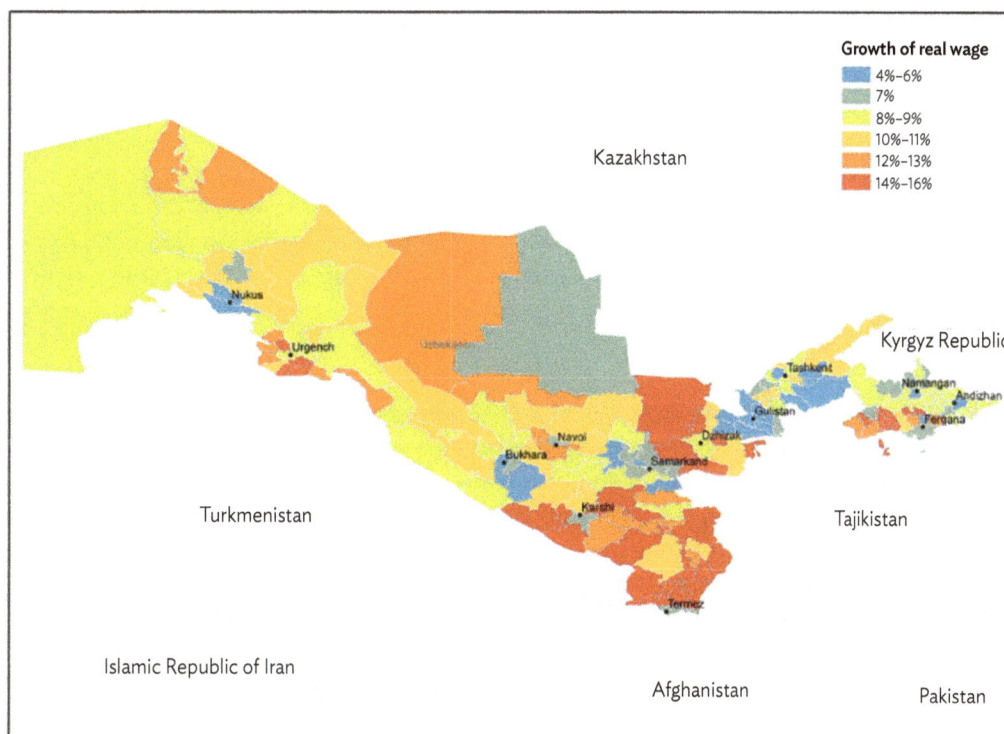

Source: S. Lall and M. Lebrand. 2019. *Who Wins, Who Loses? Understanding the Spatially Differentiated Effects of the Belt and Road Initiative. Policy Research Working Paper* 8806. Washington, DC: World Bank.

According to a World Bank study, the expected local economic impacts of transport corridors will cause a reduction in transport costs for tradable goods, coupled with an increase in the value of local land to accommodate demand from trade and logistics, employment opportunities, wages and welfare, and the value of non-tradable goods (footnote 25). To fully capture such economic benefits, however, trade facilitation policies, border improvements, and local infrastructure upgrades are needed, as well as a policy that allows labor to move in pursuit of new employment opportunities—the latter now being accomplished through the abolishment of the *propiska* system across the national territory. Cross-border trade facilitation could have deep spillover effects, rebalancing regional development and urbanization.

Large urban centers that are attractive to workers and well-connected agricultural districts would benefit from these transport corridor investments. Urban centers such as Tashkent, Bukhara, and Samarkand would keep on attracting the largest number of workers. Similarly, the agricultural regions of Djizzak, Karshi, Fergana, and Termez would also attract a large number of workers and benefit from large welfare gains. Indeed, regions in the south and east of the country have the potential to increase scale and specialization by expanding agricultural production in traditional crops (such as cotton) and in horticulture (footnote 25).

There is a clear opportunity to harmonize industrial policy, as well as transport and trade policy, with an urbanization strategy that addresses comprehensively the challenges of balancing regional development by reinforcing regional growth poles. Secondary cities, and not only the capital and its region, must be able to absorb the excess labor force that will inevitably exit the agriculture sector, as the sector too is being modernized and restructured. Job creation in urban areas would also ensure the country's capacity to retain and benefit from its full labor force rather than exporting it, as it does with two million citizens currently working abroad. Such goals are clearly stated in all of the government decrees and strategy documents quoted in Section II.1 and ought to be driving the urbanization agenda of the next decade, to 2030. Urban planning for all cities should be made over the long term, taking into account real population growth and planned economic development.

Expanding Residential Housing Construction

Increased rural to urban migration could offer huge opportunities to create value in the housing sector if current hurdles are lifted. Innovative ways have been put in place to support developers and construction companies, and appropriate financing mechanisms have been devised. A substantial increase in the production of affordable urban housing units would not only facilitate urbanization, but also generate economic returns in terms of job creation, supply chain spillovers, and additional contribution of the construction sector to the country's GDP (estimated at 6.5% of GDP in 2019).

Investments in residential constructions could also become countercyclical measures, given the likely slowdown that the main sectors of the Uzbek economy will experience in the short- to medium-term on account of the contraction of external demand for its commodities due to the COVID-19 crisis and its aftermath. However, new public policies would need to be developed to address the complexity of the housing sector in a way that has not been done up to now. The system of state subsidies would have to be reformed to ensure a greater role of the financial sector and more equitable benefits for low-income households.

Green and Resilient Cities

Increasing Urban Density

Urban land privatization, if accomplished with a market orientation, would lead to the establishment of a "pyramid" of land-values that would likely see the highest ones in the center of the city, and the lowest ones at its periphery, leading to higher central densities. However, appropriate land-use planning and zoning are needed to achieve a compact urban development, contain the overall urban footprint of Tashkent and secondary cities, and favor urban redevelopment of existing areas over greenfield projects.

Urban master plans would have to reflect an integrated vision of urban growth which benefits all residents and economic actors, while preserving urban efficiency and capturing agglomeration benefits. Compact urban form implies a careful review of the location of urban functions, to minimize vehicle miles traveled through appropriate mixed-use development favoring the proximity of residential areas with productive and commercial ones. Improving the quality of the housing stock would create the opportunity to redesign neighborhoods; introduce tertiary roads, pedestrian, and bike lanes; upgrade streets and pavements; and improve urban infrastructure and services.

Achieving Sustainability and Urban Resilience in a Post-COVID-19 Context

Cities in Uzbekistan face challenges that have been further aggravated by COVID-19. Holistic and integrated development approaches will be critical in strengthening resilience to future shocks and stresses, improving public health, and facilitating economic recovery. Investments will need to prioritize core urban services in critical areas of primary health, education, urban services and social infrastructure (i.e., water, sanitation, solid waste, heating, transport), affordable housing, and economic activity (i.e., job training, local investment), among others, which would benefit the poor and women most impacted by the pandemic.[94]

Urban planning plays a major role in balancing such various interests, while preserving the public good of well-functioning cities. Public spaces, in particular, are important for the citizens' welfare as urban density increases. Urban livability is a result of concerted policies pursuing the upgrading of the urban environment and improvements in public health via better management of solid waste, sewerage systems, and industrial pollution. The potential for urban sustainability and resilience can be further pursued with the scaling up of renewable energy and the introduction of early warning systems for flood and seismic risks and for heat waves.

Equitable and Inclusive Cities

Land Privatization

After independence, Uzbekistan granted its citizens with private ownership of housing via an equitable transfer of state properties to individual households. Current community expectations as to land privatization were gauged from the "Listening to the Citizens of Uzbekistan" survey conducted by the World Bank together with the Development Strategy Center and with guidance from the State Statistics Committee and other government partners. One of the survey's findings is that 93% of the residents believe that they should own urban land (footnote 5). Hence, it is expected that the reform or urban land ownership should benefit all Uzbek citizens.

The land privatization program is an important component of making Uzbek cities more equitable and inclusive, together with the termination of the *propiska* system. Privatizing land properties would create and distribute wealth to households, and unlock opportunities for economic development by the private sector. The timing and sequencing of the reforms related to labor mobility, land privatization, and boosting residential construction will be crucial in determining their success, and in ensuring equitable distribution of the related welfare benefits.

---

94   ADB. 2020. *Livable Cities: Post-COVID-19 New Normal*. Manila.

Alternatives to land privatization could be explored, including long-term leases (e.g., 30, 60, 99 years) as done in Singapore. While such an approach generally results in less government revenues, it offers the government more flexibility to plan for future urban changes requiring redevelopment when the leases expire.

Citizen Participation in Urban Redevelopment

Currently, there is no strong mechanism for public participation in the urban planning process to ensure development is inclusive and responsive to citizen and business needs. A reformed urban planning system can adopt consultation mechanisms whereby area plans are designed with the communities, and with the residents' and public interests in mind, in addition to the area's market potential.

Beyond consultations, urban residents would be empowered to become actors of urban redevelopment by collectively investing their land and housing properties in new residential projects. Once the privatization of urban land are completed, urban redevelopment schemes should be adopted to allow the benefits from the operations to be equitably distributed rather than captured by sector operators.

Opportunities for Further Engagement

ADB is currently preparing its first integrated urban development project, slated for approval in 2022. In addition to its benefits, the project will also be a conduit for ADB to engage more deeply in the urban sector. ADB will collaborate with the national institutions in charge of urbanization and urban development and expand its dialogue with the government in identifying specific areas for further support in the context of the future country partnership strategy. Coordination with key development partners active in urban development will be pursued to harmonize policy recommendations and coordinate operational support. The following are possible areas for further engagement:

- **Enhancing city and regional competitiveness**. The government could benefit from ADB's technical assistance in articulating the specific policies to align economic development strategies with urbanization based on the comparative advantages of cities and regions. Such technical assistance would chiefly address cities located along transport corridors, close to free economic zones, and with transborder trade opportunities. It would identify policy measures and infrastructure investments that would enhance agglomeration benefits and promote urban job creation.

- **Supporting decentralization and financial sustainability**. ADB could support the government in its efforts to move toward greater decentralization and to empower municipalities to become more fiscally autonomous. Support may also be given through institutional capacity building on budget transparency, municipal financing, and public financial management. A rule-based transparent transfer system could be developed to foster efficiency and prevent political manipulation or abrupt disruptions to the income that municipalities and SNGs expect to receive. Greater efficiency in SNGs could be promoted by establishing the link between expenditure and revenue resources.

- **Strengthening urban governance and institutions**. ADB could support the government in developing greater responsiveness to local citizens. Better urban governance at the local level includes citizen participation and community outreach and supporting women in areas of livelihood. Strengthening central level institutions and city governments will help them better manage urban development. Local governments can make evidence-based decisions and work effectively on integrated urban planning when their systems are modernized and equipped with data generation capabilities and digital technologies (e.g., geographic information system).

- **Meeting urban infrastructure needs**. ADB has been consistently present and has a large portfolio of operations in all key sectors of municipal infrastructure. It is thus a trusted government partner that could facilitate the identification of PPP opportunities for the provision of urban infrastructure and management of urban services. PPPs will help close the infrastructure investment gap. To sustain previous and ongoing engagements, the technical and financial performance of utility companies would be addressed as key components.

- **Improving urban livability**. ADB could support Tashkent and/or some of the secondary cities with city-specific audits of their risk exposure to natural hazards and impacts of climate change, as well as local pollution and public health assessments related to environmental concerns. Such audits would eventually become critical inputs in preparing urban plans. These would also address public spaces as areas of particular attention, providing connectivity and integration among urban components and improving the citizens' quality of life.

APPENDIX 1
Population, Urban Population ('000), Rate of Urbanization in 2000, 2010, 2019, and Growth Projections to 2030

Region	2000 Total ('000)	2000 Urban	2000 % Urban	2010 Total ('000)	2010 Urban	2010 % Urban	2019 Total ('000)	2019 Urban	2019 % Urban	2010-2019 CAGR (%)	2030 Projections Total ('000)	2030 Urban	2030 % Urban
Republic of Karakalpakstan	1,503	724	48.2	1,632	820	50.3	1,870	918	49.1	1.25	2,208	1,053	47.7
Andijan	2,186	658	30.1	2,549	1,358	53.3	3,067	1,604	52.3	1.86	3,845	1,964	51.1
Bukhara	1,419	441	31.1	1,613	622	38.6	1,895	701	37.0	1.34	2,308	812	35.2
Jizzakh	975	295	30.2	1,117	527	47.2	1,352	635	46.9	2.09	1,709	796	46.6
Kashkadarya	2,167	551	25.4	2,616	1,136	43.4	3,213	1,384	43.1	2.22	4,131	1,761	42.6
Navoi	783	317	40.4	852	421	49.4	980	478	48.8	1.43	1,162	559	48.1
Namangan	1,924	723	37.6	2,259	1,459	64.6	2,753	1,778	64.6	2.22	3,506	2,263	64.5
Samarkand	2,670	724	27.1	3,119	1,160	37.2	3,799	1,415	37.2	2.23	4,834	1,802	37.3
Surkhandarya	1,737	345	19.9	2,075	768	37.0	2,570	911	35.4	1.91	3,338	1,122	33.6
Syrdarya	642	206	32.1	714	295	41.3	830	355	42.8	2.08	997	445	44.7
Tashkent Region + City	4,493	3,092	68.8	4,820	3,528	73.2	5,408	3,937	72.8	1.23	6,226	4,504	72.3
Fergana	2,664	776	29.1	3,075	1,803	58.6	3,683	2,083	56.5	1.62	4,593	2,484	54.1
Khorezm	1,324	315	23.8	1,562	530	33.9	1,836	610	33.2	1.58	2,237	725	32.4
Total	24,488	9,166	37.4	28,001	14,426	51.5	33,256	16,807	50.5	1.71	41,093	20,291	49.4

CAGR = compounded annual growth rate.

Notes: The population figures for the City of Tashkent have been merged with the ones for the Tashkent Region. This allows for a better assessment of the actual concentration of urban population within the regional boundaries. The low compounded annual growth rates (CAGR) for the combined Tashkent City and Region data belies the distortion of official figures which do not account for informal migration into the capital city. This distortion applies to all reference years, 2030 projections included.

The considerable increase in urbanization rates across most regions between 2000 and 2010 is mainly due to a reclassification of formally rural districts into urban districts in 2009 (Maps A1.1 and A1.2). Since 2010, the CAGR for most regions has been on the decline, resulting in reduction in urbanization from 51.5% in 2010 to 50.4% in 2019 (Map A1.3). If this trend continues, the projection for 2030 would be a further decline in the urbanization rate to 49.4% (Map A1.4). While the lifting of the propiska system is likely to result in an increase in rural-to-urban migration, it would be challenging to reach the government target of 60% urbanization by 2030. Various dynamics, whether policy–driven or not, could modify such trends in the course of the coming decade. Further investments in making cities more attractive for businesses and citizens alike will be needed to encourage an increase in rural-to-urban migration.

Source: Uzbekistan State Commission on Statistics.

Map A1.1: Uzbekistan's Urban Population in 2000, by Region

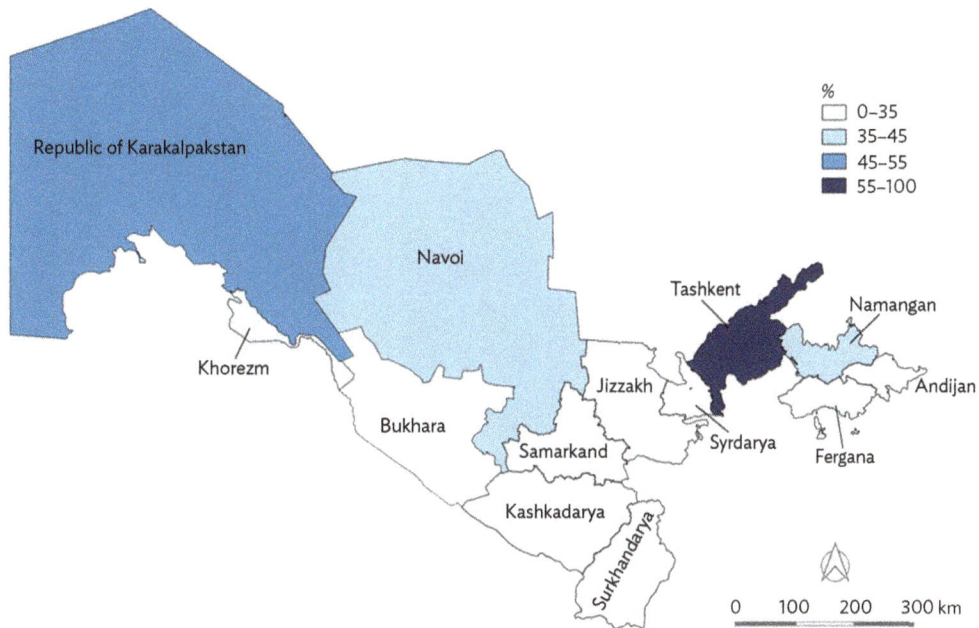

%
- ☐ 0–35
- 35–45
- 45–55
- 55–100

Republic of Karakalpakstan

Navoi

Tashkent

Namangan

Khorezm

Bukhara

Jizzakh

Andijan

Samarkand

Syrdarya

Fergana

Kashkadarya

Surkhandarya

0   100   200   300 km

Source: Based on population data from State Committee of the Republic of Uzbekistan on Statistics (map by the Asian Development Bank).

Map A1.2: Uzbekistan's Urban Population in 2010, by Region

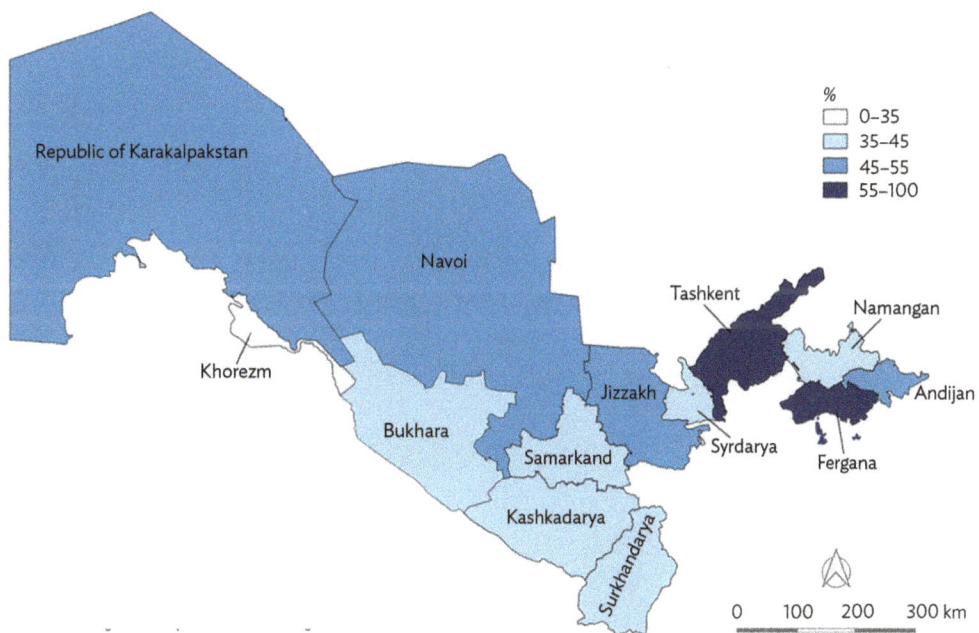

%
- ☐ 0–35
- 35–45
- 45–55
- 55–100

Republic of Karakalpakstan

Navoi

Tashkent

Namangan

Khorezm

Bukhara

Jizzakh

Andijan

Samarkand

Syrdarya

Fergana

Kashkadarya

Surkhandarya

0   100   200   300 km

Source: Based on population data from State Committee of the Republic of Uzbekistan on Statistics (map by the Asian Development Bank).

Map A1.3: Uzbekistan's Urban Population in 2019, by Region

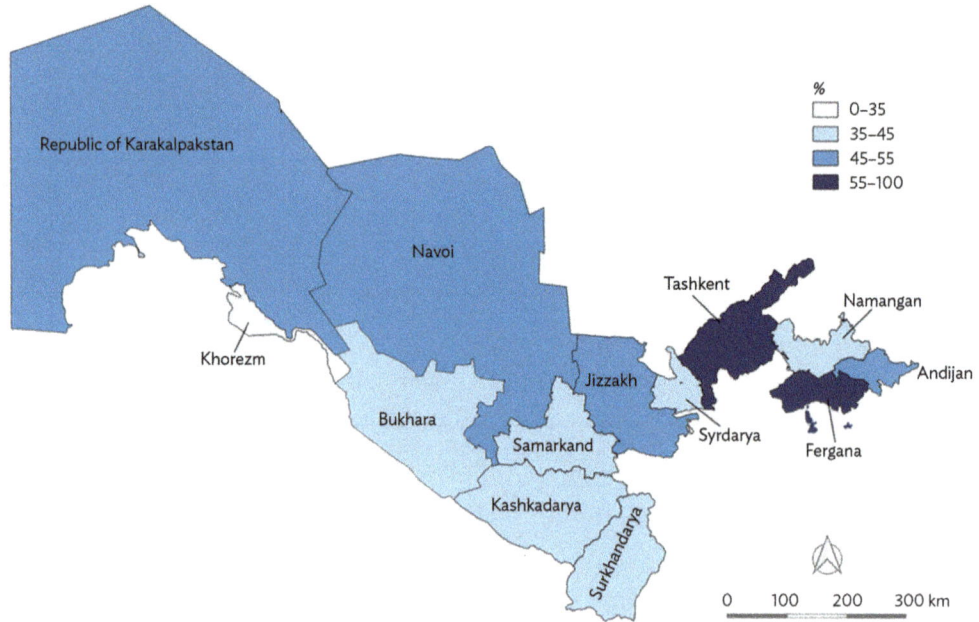

%
- 0–35
- 35–45
- 45–55
- 55–100

Republic of Karakalpakstan

Navoi

Khorezm

Bukhara

Samarkand

Kashkadarya

Surkhandarya

Jizzakh

Tashkent

Syrdarya

Namangan

Andijan

Fergana

0   100   200   300 km

Source: Based on population data from State Committee of the Republic of Uzbekistan on Statistics (map by the Asian Development Bank).

Map A1.4: Uzbekistan's Urban Population in 2030, by Region
(status quo growth)

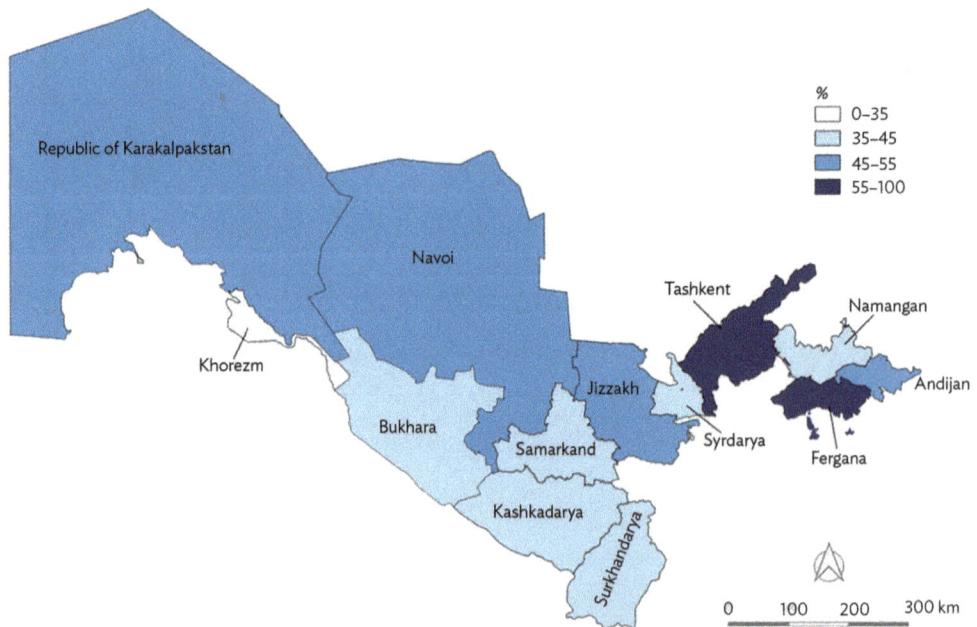

%
- 0–35
- 35–45
- 45–55
- 55–100

Republic of Karakalpakstan

Navoi

Khorezm

Bukhara

Samarkand

Kashkadarya

Surkhandarya

Jizzakh

Tashkent

Syrdarya

Namangan

Andijan

Fergana

0   100   200   300 km

Source: Based on population data from State Committee of the Republic of Uzbekistan on Statistics (map by the Asian Development Bank).

Map A2.1: Uzbekistan Fast Facts, 2017

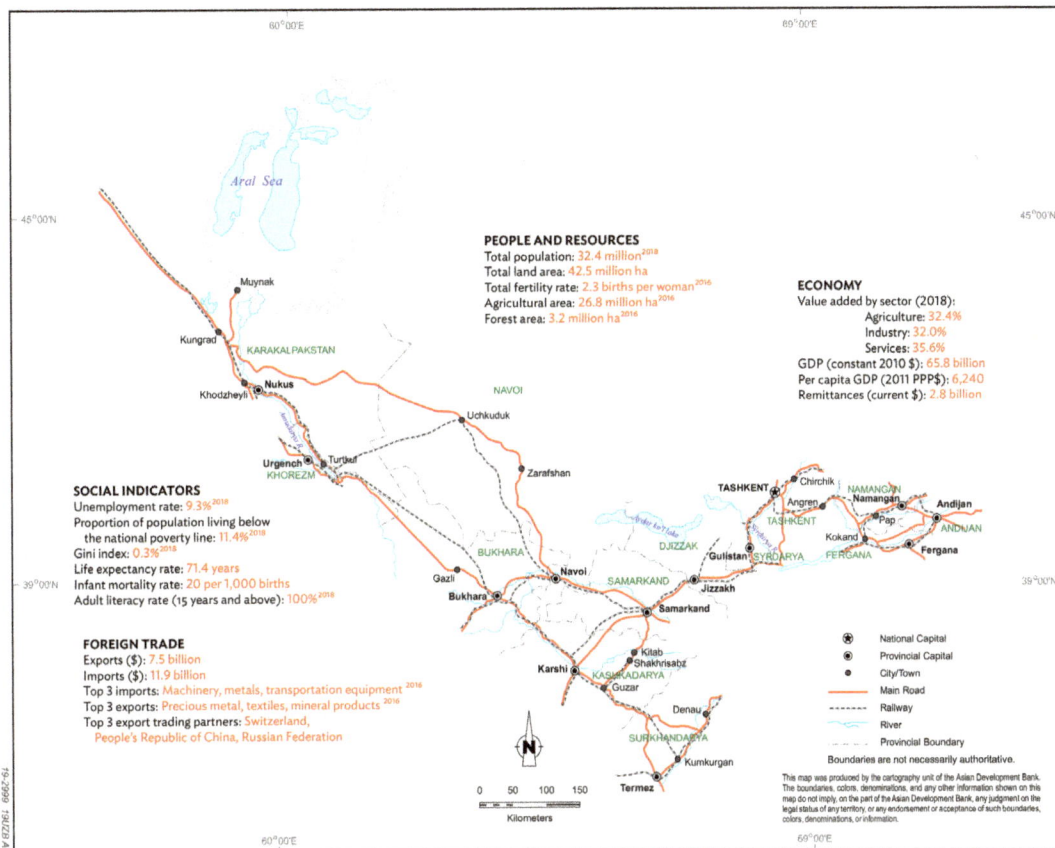

PEOPLE AND RESOURCES
Total population: 32.4 million [2018]
Total land area: 42.5 million ha
Total fertility rate: 2.3 births per woman [2016]
Agricultural area: 26.8 million ha [2016]
Forest area: 3.2 million ha [2016]

ECONOMY
Value added by sector (2018):
Agriculture: 32.4%
Industry: 32.0%
Services: 35.6%
GDP (constant 2010 $): 65.8 billion
Per capita GDP (2011 PPP$): 6,240
Remittances (current $): 2.8 billion

SOCIAL INDICATORS
Unemployment rate: 9.3% [2018]
Proportion of population living below
the national poverty line: 11.4% [2018]
Gini index: 0.3% [2018]
Life expectancy rate: 71.4 years
Infant mortality rate: 20 per 1,000 births
Adult literacy rate (15 years and above): 100% [2018]

FOREIGN TRADE
Exports ($): 7.5 billion
Imports ($): 11.9 billion
Top 3 imports: Machinery, metals, transportation equipment [2016]
Top 3 exports: Precious metal, textiles, mineral products [2016]
Top 3 export trading partners: Switzerland,
People's Republic of China, Russian Federation

National Capital
Provincial Capital
City/Town
Main Road
Railway
River
Provincial Boundary
Boundaries are not necessarily authoritative.

This map was produced by the cartography unit of the Asian Development Bank.
The boundaries, colors, denominations, and any other information shown on this
map do not imply, on the part of the Asian Development Bank, any judgment on the
legal status of any territory, or any endorsement or acceptance of such boundaries,
colors, denominations, or information.

Aral Sea
Muynak
Kungrad
KARAKALPAKSTAN
Nukus
Khodzheyli
NAVOI
Uchkuduk
Urgench Turtkul
KHOREZM
Zarafshan
TASHKENT
Chirchik
NAMANGAN
Angren Namangan
TASHKENT Andijan
Pap ANDIJAN
Kokand
BUKHARA
DJIZZAK
FERGANA
Fergana
Gazli Navoi
Gulistan SYRDARYA
SAMARKAND
Bukhara
Jizzakh
Samarkand
Kilab
Shakhrisabz
KASHKADARYA
Karshi
Guzar
Denau
N
SURKHANDARYA
0 50 100 150
Kumkurgan
Termez
Kilometers

60°00'E
60°00'E
60°00'E
69°00'E
45°00'N
45°00'N
48°00'N
39°00'N
39°00'N

Source: Asian Development Bank. 2020.

Map A2.2: Central Asia Regional Economic Cooperation Program Designated Rail Corridors

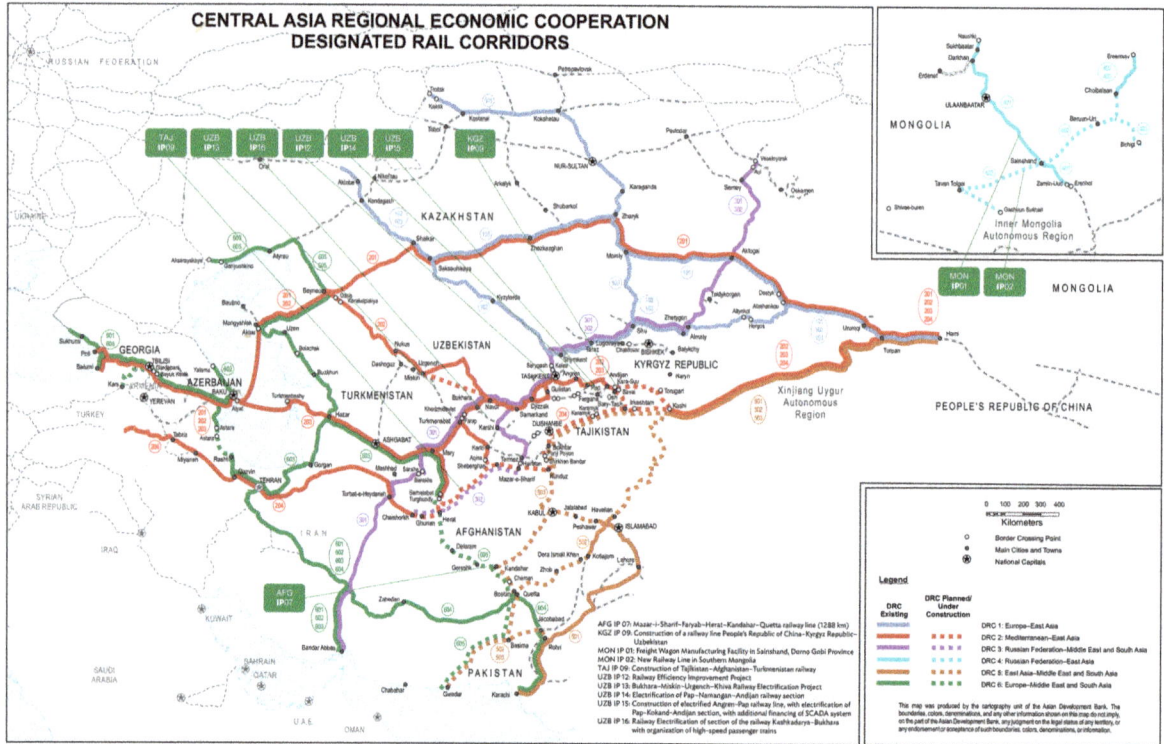

Source: www.carecprogram.org.

APPENDIX 3
Central Government Institutions

Agency	Role and Functions in Urban Sector
Ministry of Economic Development and Poverty Reduction	• Formulate strategies for development of industries and allocation of production forces to promote balanced territorial development, improvement of competitiveness, and promotion of economic growth. • Promote implementation of national urbanization policy, ensure synergy between urbanization policy and industrial policy, develop housing and public utilities in urban areas, and promote efficient land use. • Coordinate formulation and implementation of national, sectoral, and territorial development programs, including development of industries, transport communications, public utilities, health care and education, and employment promotion.
Ministry of Finance	• Improve budget process, promote municipal finance reform (including decentralization), and allocate transfers to municipalities. • Conduct financial planning for government investment programs, and for accumulation and distribution of funds for operation and maintenance of government assets in various sectors. • Review and approve investment projects financed by government funds and through loans from international financial institutions (IFIs). • Consult and coordinate municipalities regarding mobilization of additional local budget revenues.
Ministry of Investments and Foreign Trade	• Coordinate formulation and implementation of government development and investment program, both sectoral and territorial and promote private sector investments, including foreign direct investments. • Coordinate cooperation of government agencies with IFIs and development partners and support development and implementation of investment projects in various sectors. • Coordinate development of foreign economic relations, including promotion of export potentials. • Support development of international transport and transit, logistics networks, and economic corridors.
Ministry of Construction	• Formulate and approve city master plans, and the general scheme of population settlement through specialized institutions and organizations coordinated by the ministry. • Monitor implementation of master plans; control the enforcement of national legislation in urban planning, land use, research and development, and construction. • Participate in the formulation of national, sectoral, and territorial socioeconomic development programs. • Formulate medium- and long-term government development programs in architecture, design, planning, and construction. • Review and approve construction and investments projects. • Promote introduction of resource efficient technologies and approaches in urban planning and construction sector. • Lead the improvement of national laws and regulations in urban planning and construction.

Agency	Role and Functions in Urban Sector
Ministry of Housing and Communal Services	• Coordinate homeowners' associations to maintain existing urban housing and nearby public spaces. • Formulate and implement rehabilitation and reconstruction works in the urban housing sector. • Operate the special fund for development of housing and communal services. • Formulate and implement government investment programs in water supply and sanitation, heating, and hot water supply, including projects supported by IFIs. • Coordinate activities related to development and implementation of investment projects in water supply and sanitation, heating, and hot water supply.
State Committee on Land Resources, Geodesy, Cartography and State Cadaster (recently abolished with responsibilities transferred to the newly established Cadaster Agency under the State Tax Authority)	• Maintain registry of land and buildings, among others. • Develop GIS-based systems for urban areas (e.g., lands, infrastructure, roads) and implement topographical surveys for construction projects. • Identify physical borders of administrative units, including urban settlements. • Participate in privatization of land together with other stakeholders and establish mechanism for identifying the market value of property and land. • Assess agricultural land value (expansion of cities).
Ministry of Energy	• Formulate national programs in the energy sector and allocate generation capacities and transmission facilities. • Coordinate national companies in electricity, oil and gas sectors, including distribution networks in urban and rural areas. • Lead the promotion of renewable energy and energy-efficient technologies.
Ministry of Transport	• Formulate and implement national policy for automobile, railways, and airways transport. • Develop integrated national transport and logistics system and promote new national and international corridors.
State Committee for Ecology and Environment Protection	• Protect and improve natural environment in cities. • Maintain green spaces in cities. • Manage solid waste. • Review and eco-assess construction and investment projects. • Promote green energy technologies. • Monitor and assess ecological conditions in the cities and assess urban environmental impacts.
Ministry of Women and Mahalla Support	• Develop and implement unified state policy in the areas of family support, women, and the elderly. • Protect their legal interests and rights. • Establish cooperation with community-driven, self-governing institutions.
State Committee on Tourism Development	• Formulate and implement tourism development. • Attract investments into tourism industry. • Develop tourist infrastructure (transport, communications, public utilities, hotels, restaurants) and protect cultural heritage sites.
Ministry of Information Technology and Communications	• Develop national ICT networks and coordinate with the National Uztelecom Company. • Support and promote e-government projects and programs in various sectors.
Ministry of Culture	• Protect cultural heritage and rehabilitate and conserve heritage sites and objects. • Review construction and investments projects affecting cultural and historic heritage. • Develop and maintain national parks, museums, and libraries—including via promotion of public–private partnerships (PPPs).

Agency	Role and Functions in Urban Sector
Agency for Management of State Assets	• Privatize government shares in state-owned enterprises, including public utilities companies. • Manage infrastructure companies, particularly in telecom, transport, and finance.
Agency for Public–Private Partnership Development	• Develop rules and regulations on PPP. • Pilot and promote PPP projects in the urban sector. • Review and approve PPP agreements.
Ministry of Healthcare, including State Sanitary and Epidemiological Service	• Assess health situation and forecast demand for health-care services over the medium and long term. • Hold and manage government assets in public health care (emergency care, hospitals). • Promote PPP in the health-care sector. • Promote healthy lifestyle. • Monitor the quality of natural environment and assess its impact on people's health. • Review construction and investment projects. • Check quality and safety of urban services in water supply and sanitation, and in solid waste management.
Ministry on Emergency Situations	• Prevent emergencies, and protect lives and people's well-being and protect public and private property. • Develop and implement emergency plans. • Review and assess construction and investments projects.

GIS = geographic information system, ICT = information and communication technology.
Source: Asian Development Bank.

APPENDIX 4
Legal Underpinnings of the Status of Municipalities

The content for Appendix 4 is taken from the constitution, decrees, and resolutions of the Government of Uzbekistan.

1. Fundamental Principles of Municipalities as per Constitutional Articles

(i)　The responsibilities of the municipalities shall include:

- ensuring legality, legal order, and security of citizens;
- dealing with economic, social, and cultural development within their territories;
- formation and implementation of the local budget, determination of the local taxes and fees, and formation of non-budget funds;
- direction of the municipal economy;
- environmental protection;
- ensuring the registration of civil status acts; and
- adoption of normative acts and their implementation within the frames which would not contradict the Constitution and legislation of the Republic of Uzbekistan.[1]

(ii)　The municipalities shall enforce the laws of the Republic of Uzbekistan, decrees of the President, decisions of the higher bodies of state authority, and participate in the discussion of matters of national and local significance. The decisions of the higher bodies adopted within their competence shall be binding on the subordinate bodies. The term of service of the Peoples' Council (Kengash) representatives and Mayors (Khokims) is five years.[2]

(iii)　The Governor of the region, district, city and town Mayors shall serve as the head of the representative and executive power of his relevant territory. The Governor of the region and the Mayor of the Tashkent city shall be appointed/outpost of his position by the President of the Republic of Uzbekistan. The Mayors of districts and cities shall be appointed/outposted of their positions by the Governor of the region and the city of Tashkent, as applicable, and approved by the relevant People's Council representatives. The Mayor of towns which are subordinated to district centers shall be appointed/outposted of their positions by the Mayor of the district center and approved by the district Peoples' Council representatives.[3]

(iv)　The Governor of [the] region, district, city, and town Mayors shall execute their relevant power in accordance with the principle of one-man management and shall bear personal responsibility for

---

[1]　Government of Uzbekistan. 1992. *Constitution of the Republic of Uzbekistan*. Chapter 21, Article 100.

[2]　Government of Uzbekistan. 1992. *Constitution of the Republic of Uzbekistan*. Chapter 21, Article 101.

[3]　Government of Uzbekistan. 1992. *Constitution of the Republic of Uzbekistan*. Chapter 21, Article 102.

decisions and actions of bodies subordinated to relevant Mayor, as applicable. The Governor of [the] region, district, city and town Mayors shall report to the relevant People's Council on major and actual matters of the socio-economic development of the region, district and city/town. Based on it, the People's Council representatives shall adopt relevant decisions and recommend actions. The organization of the work and authorities of Mayors and local Peoples' Council representatives, as well as the procedure for the elections to the local Peoples' Council shall be regulated by law.[4]

(v)   The Governor/Mayor within his vested powers shall adopt decisions, which are binding on all enterprises, institutions, organizations, associations, as well as officials and citizens on the relevant territory.[5]

(vi) Self-governing bodies in settlements, kishlaks and auls, as well as in makhallas of cities, towns, settlements, kishlaks and auls, shall be assemblies of citizens electing chairman (*aksakal*). The procedure for the elections, organization of the work, and authorities of self-governing bodies shall be regulated by law.

2.   Local Governance Organizational and Financial Management

(i)   In recent years, significant work has been carried out in the Republic to improve the activities of local government bodies, aimed at the integrated development of territories, improving the local executive structure, which is capable of timely and effective resolution of local problems. At the same time, a study of the real situation in the city of Tashkent indicates the presence of systemic problems and shortcomings that hinder the accelerated growth and modernization of economic sectors, attracting investment, the development of the social sphere, and the prompt resolution of pressing problems of the population. Among them:

- first, there is no integrated approach and close interaction of Governors and their deputies with the territorial divisions of government bodies in solving the socio-economic problems of the region;

- second, a number of unusual tasks and functions that have no organizational, legal, and financial mechanisms for implementation are entrusted to local government bodies, as a result of which Governors/Mayors create separate quasi-state enterprises and organizations endowed with administrative and managerial functions;

- third, the presence of a large number of interdepartmental territorial collegial bodies (commissions, councils) endowed with state-power authority, leads to a substitution of tasks and functions of local executive authorities, erosion of responsibility for decisions made and achievement of specific results;

- fourth, the lack of an approved master plan of the city of Tashkent leads to disordered construction, does not allow to determine the further expansion of the activities of business entities, and also inhibits the rapid social and economic development of the capital, taking into account the comprehensive distribution of social facilities and the expansion of engineering and communication networks;

- fifth, the current procedure for material incentives for local executive employees does not correspond to the volume of tasks, functions and responsibilities assigned to them, which affects the efficiency of their work;

- sixth, the mechanisms of People's Council representatives and public control are not involved at the proper level, the current procedure for organizing the activities of the People's Council Representatives do not fully provide control over the activities of local executive bodies.[6]

---

[4]   Government of Uzbekistan. 1992. *Constitution of the Republic of Uzbekistan. Chapter 21*, Article 103.
[5]   Government of Uzbekistan. 1992. *Constitution of the Republic of Uzbekistan. Chapter 21*, Article 104.
[6]   Government of Uzbekistan. 2018. *Presidential Decree of the Republic of Uzbekistan No. UP-5517 "On legal experiment on the implementation [of] a special management order in Tashkent city."*

(ii) To ensure sustainable financing of the integrated development of territories on the basis of a radical strengthening of the revenue base and decentralization of local budgets, further improving intergovernmental relations, strengthening the financial independence of local government bodies and increasing their responsibility for implementing specific targeted measures to expand the tax potential by promoting the development of small business and private entrepreneurship, creating new jobs and providing employment, accelerated development of engineering and communications, road transport and social infrastructure, a relevant Presidential Decree was adopted.[7]

(iii) In accordance with the Strategy for Actions on Priority Directions for the Development of the Republic of Uzbekistan for 2017–2021 and to radically strengthen the revenue base of local budgets, reduce their dependence on deductions from higher budgets, increase on this basis the independence and responsibility of local government bodies for unconditional provision [and for] the implementation of strategically important investment projects for the modernization and technical updating of the housing and communal, transport, communication and social infrastructure, a relevant Presidential Decree was adopted.[8]

(iv) Establishing the "Prosperous neighborhood" (*obod makhalla*) Fund to finance the construction, repair, and landscaping works in city. Funds are generated from the following sources:

- transfers allocated from the republican budget of the Republic of Uzbekistan;
- budget of the Republic of Karakalpakstan, local budgets of regions and the city of Tashkent and their additional funds;
- funds of the Mahalla public charity fund, funds received from community work days and charity events, sponsorship of organizations;
- funds of the Public Works Fund under the Ministry of Employment and Labor Relations of the Republic of Uzbekistan;
- grants from international financial institutions and foreign states; and
- funds of initiative entrepreneurs and other sources not prohibited by law.

Funds are allocated to:

- improving the guaranteed provision of the population with drinking water and sewage, heating networks, and the creation of the necessary infrastructure for the collection and removal of household waste;
- adaptation of the irrigation and irrigation network, based on the available water for irrigation, modernization of collector and drainage networks, and lowering the level of groundwater;
- construction and repair of mahalla roads and pedestrian paths, improvement and greening of the roadside territory, and creation of external lighting systems;
- priority construction, reconstruction, and repair of mahallas of buildings and structures of state preschool educational institutions, comprehensive schools, medical organizations, cultural organizations, physical education, and sports;
- providing material and financial assistance to families in need of social support, in the repair of their housing, as well as providing the population with building materials in a preferential manner;

---

[7] Government of Uzbekistan. 2017. Presidential Decree of the Republic of Uzbekistan No. UP-5283 "On additional measures to increase financial authority in places, strengthening liability of taxes, and financial authorities for completeness [of] arrivals in local budgets."

[8] Government of Uzbekistan. 2017. Presidential Decree of the Republic of Uzbekistan No. UP-5075 "On measures to extend powers of state authority bodies in place in the formation of local budgets."

- the construction of "mahalla centers," including the mahalla premises, convenient and inexpensive pharmacies at medical institutions, the necessary points of consumer services, as well as playgrounds, small recreation parks; and
- financing of additional activities for the implementation of the program "Obod Makhalla."[9]

(v) To entrust to the Council of Ministers of the Republic of Karakalpakstan, Regional Mayor offices and the city of Tashkent, districts, and cities['] Mayors: (Paragraph as amended by the Decree of the President of the Republic of Uzbekistan dated 2017)

- increasing local budget revenues due to the full coverage of taxpayers on their territory and increasing tax collection, creating new production enterprises, restoring the production activities of economically insolvent, non-working enterprises;
- fulfillment of approved revenue forecasts of the respective local budgets, timely and full financing of expenses within the framework of the legislation, including wages and equivalent payments;
- increase in wages of employees of budgetary organizations in the amounts established by Decrees of the President of the Republic of Uzbekistan on increasing wages and other regulatory legal acts; and
- preventing the introduction of additional staffing units in budgetary organizations in excess of statutory standards approved by law.[10]

(vi) To increase the efficiency of attracting foreign direct investment in the infrastructural development of the city of Tashkent, to widely inform foreign investors about the opportunities and potential of the capital, to increase the responsibility of regional Governorates for creating favorable conditions for attracting foreign investment and implementing investment projects, the Cabinet of Ministers decides to determine the main tasks of the Tashkent city Mayor, Mayor of the districts in attracting of foreign direct investment:

- improving the investment climate for doing business in Tashkent city;
- creating infrastructure for the development of high-tech industries and products with high added value, including in small industrial zones and technology parks, with an increase in their production and exports;
- increasing the attractiveness of the capital as a tourist center of the region, increasing the flow of domestic and foreign tourists, creating a network of hotels of various formats, as well as developing medical tourism;
- the opening of branches of leading international higher educational institutions, the implementation of the construction, reconstruction, and technical re-equipment of health-care institutions, including using public–private partnership mechanisms;
- attraction of multinational companies, large international financial corporations, development of the capital as a regional financial center;
- attracting private investment in the construction of modern office premises and housing complexes with the provision of their appropriate infrastructure, further development of construction in certain areas of the capital with the introduction of smart city and green city systems;
- development of engineering and communal infrastructure, improving the quality and accessibility of utilities, the introduction of energy-efficient technologies and accelerating the connection to the engineering and communications networks of enterprises with foreign investment.[11]

---

[9] Government of Uzbekistan. 2018. Presidential Decree of the Republic of Uzbekistan No. UP-5467 "On the program Obod Makhalla." 27 June.
[10] Government of Uzbekistan. 2017. Resolution of the President of the Republic of Uzbekistan PP-3042 "Extension of authority in place and increasing their responsibility for [the] formation of local budget income." 6 July.
[11] Government of Uzbekistan. 2019. Cabinet of Ministers' Resolution No. 4. 4 January.

According to the Law of the Republic of Uzbekistan "On the procedure for resolving issues of the administrative-territorial structure," as well as for the accelerated socio-economic development of regions, the full use of reserves and opportunities of cities, ensuring coordinated activities of government and local executive bodies on effective solutions, strategic and most important perspective tasks in this direction:

(i)   To establish a Department of socio-economic development of cities of republican subordination in the executive structure of the Cabinet of Ministers of Republic of Uzbekistan (hereinafter referred to as the Department) and determine that its activities are coordinated directly by the Prime Minister of the Republic of Uzbekistan.

(ii) Form the staff units of the Department by reducing 2 staff units in the structure of the administration of the Tashkent regional khokimiyat and 10 staff units in the structure of the Tourism Development Department of the Tashkent region.

(iii) Identify the main tasks of the department:

- ensuring coordinated activities of local government and executive authorities in effectively addressing the challenges of the future development of the cities of Angren, Bekabad, Almalyk and Chirchik, Tashkent region, the city of Shirin, Syrdarya region, the city of Zarafshan, Navoi region and the village of Shargun, Saryasi district, Surkhandarya region;

- development and organization of the implementation of practical measures to radically increase the competitiveness of urban economies, develop innovative activities, strengthen support for exporting enterprises, and comprehensively stimulate the participation of farms and business entities in export;

- taking necessary measures to make full use of the untapped reserves and opportunities of cities, identify labor and production potentials, make effective use of available mineral and raw material resources, labor, and production potentials, expand the revenue side of local budgets, implement measures to reduce subvention, and increase the financial stability of enterprises;

- providing, together with government bodies and business associations, the development and implementation of program activities for the accelerated development of the industrial potential of cities, the creation of new high-tech industries to deepen the industrial processing of mineral raw materials and agricultural raw materials, the organization of the production of competitive products with high added value and, on this basis, increase volumes production and range of products exported;

- drawing up proposals for the development and monitoring of the implementation of programs for the socio-economic development of cities, taking into account their peculiar features, identifying and promptly resolving problematic issues that impede their timely and high-quality execution, with adjustments to the adopted territorial programs;

- development of proposals to ensure income growth and increase the purchasing power of the urban population, saturation of the domestic consumer market, uninterrupted supply of electricity, natural gas and coal to the population, the development of education, health, culture, and sports;

- exercising systematic control over timely, full-fledged, and high-quality implementation of events in the cities within the framework of the Prosperous Mahalla program, including the development of engineering, road transport, and telecommunications infrastructure, further improvement of transport services, and a radical increase in the level and quality of housing and communal services, providing high-quality drinking water and a sanitation system, landscaping settlements, improving housing conditions, and building affordable and comfortable housing;

- attracting direct foreign investment in the urban economy, promoting the development and support of active entrepreneurship, and removing barriers to the accelerated and stable development of business entities; and

- taking effective measures to timely and fully resolve problems in the development of cities requiring solutions at the republican level with the involvement of government bodies and business associations.[12]

3.   Recent Documents

The newly drafted Presidential Decree [13] is aiming to achieve the city's development plan, its future and improving the quality to a new level, architectural planning and infrastructure to improve the appearance of the city:

- Accept for information that the development of the general plan Concept of Tashkent city till 2041 has been in process of implementation with participation of the Tashkent city Mayor office, SUE "ToshkentboshplanLITI," the company "Kentsel Renewal Center AS."
- The Master plan of the city development until 2041 (and later) in order to develop a master plan, developed by Tashkent city administration, based on the proposed concepts and to clarify the basic indicators at the expense of the city until 2041 to develop the concept of the General Plan.

The Tashkent city administration, ToshkentboshplanLITI, by 1 April 2020 shall develop the Concept of General plan of Tashkent city on the basis of the" Road map " for the further project development and approval by the Cabinet of Ministers. To develop a draft plan for Tashkent city:

- Determine the customer-municipal administration. The main project organization is SUE "TashkentboshplanLITI."
- Involve:
    - the Institute of Forecasting and Macroeconomic Research under the Ministry of Economic Development and Poverty Reduction for the preparation of documents on socio-economic development of regions;
    - JSC "Uzogirsanoatloyiha" for the preparation of documents for the development of the industrial complex, defining the promising industries and their territorial location in each structure of the city;
    - the protection of cultural heritage and Tashkent city plan to be taken into account in the development of their project for the development of the Cultural Heritage Department of the Ministry of Culture;
    - as an exception, to allow the customer and the general project organization to involve local and foreign companies, as well as specialists on the basis of direct contracts without conducting tenders for the development of the Master Plan of Tashkent city;
    - the Ministry of Construction, the Ministry of Information Technologies and Communications and the Tashkent city administration to establish a joint venture in the field of building information modeling technology (BIM), providing participation of residents of IT Park in the software and information technology park and in the development of the Tashkent Master Plan to present further for consideration of the Cabinet of Ministers.

---

[12]   Government of Uzbekistan. 2019. Presidential Order UP-5738 "On additional measures for integrated socio-economic development of cities of state subordination." 6 April.

[13]   Government of Uzbekistan. Draft Presidential Decree "On measures to develop a draft master plan for the development of Tashkent until 2041."

4. Other Normative Acts on City Development

By a separate law and other normative acts, the position, goals, and objectives of the free economic zones, districts, and cities development are determined:

Date	Title of Normative Act
Law dated 17.02.2020 N604	"On Free Economic Zones in Uzbekistan"
Presidential Decrees on Free Economic Zone	UP-4059 "On Free Economic Zone Navoi"
Presidential Decrees on Free Economic Zone	UP-4516 "On Free Economic Zone Jizzak"
Presidential Decrees on Free Economic Zone	UP-4986 "On Free Economic Zone Angren"
Presidential Decrees on Free Economic Zone	UP-4931 "On Free Economic Zones Urgut, Gijduvan, Kokand, Khazarasp"
Cabmin Resolution No. 691	"On Free Economic Zones in pharm industry"
Cabmin Resolution No. 395 20.06.2020	On measures for social and economic development and poverty reduction of the Bayaut District of the Syrdarya Region in 2020–2021
Cabmin Resolution No. 377 15.06.2020	On measures for the comprehensive socio-economic development of the Khazarasp region of the Khorezm region for 2020–2022
Cabmin Resolution No. 346 02.06.2020	On measures for integrated socio-economic development of Tuprakkala district of Khorezm region in 2020–2022
Cabmin Resolution No. 323 23.05.2020	About the complex socio-economic development of the city of Zarafshan in the Navoi region in 2020–2022
Cabmin Resolution No. 294 19.05.2020	On measures for construction and repair of housing, social and industrial infrastructure in Sardoba, Akaltin and Mirzaabad districts of Syrdarya region
Cabmin Resolution No. 268 06.05.2020	On measures to accelerate the ongoing large-scale creation and improvement work in the city of Samarkand
Cabmin Resolution No. 243 18.04.2020	On measures for the comprehensive socio-economic development of the Bozatau region of the Republic of Karakalpakstan for 2020–2021
Cabmin Resolution No. 222 14.04.2020	On measures to implement the Program for the comprehensive socio-economic development of the Denau region of the Surkhandarya region and its center in 2020–2022
Cabmin Resolution No. 160 16.03.2020	On measures for the comprehensive socio-economic development of the Altynsay district of the Surkhandarya region for 2020–2022
Cabmin Resolution No. 151 13.03.2020	On measures for integrated socio-economic development of Angren, Tashkent region in 2020–2022
Cabmin Resolution No. 152 13.03.2020	On measures for the comprehensive socio-economic development of the city of Chirchik in the Tashkent region in the period 2020–2022
Cabmin Resolution No. 149 13.03.2020	On measures for integrated socio-economic development of Almalik, Tashkent region in 2020–2022
Cabmin Resolution No. 150 13.03.2020	On measures for integrated socio-economic development of Bekabad, Tashkent region in 2020–2022

Cabmin = Cabinet of Ministers.

APPENDIX 5

International Financial Institutions and Other Development Agencies—Investments in Urban and Urban-Related Sectors, 2011–2020

Year	Project ID	Project Title	Project Cost ($)	Commitment ($)	Status
		Asian Development Bank			
2020	51034-002	Sustainable Solid-Waste Management Project	60,000,000	60,000,000	Approved
2019	53107-001	Urban Services Projects	15,000,000	15,000,000	Approved
2019	51240-001	Second Tashkent Province Water Supply Development Project	105,000,000	105,000,000	Active
2019	52317-001	Preparing Urban Development and Improvement Projects	3,000,000	3,000,000	Active
2019	51348-001	Mortgage Market Sector Development Program	200,080,000	200,080,000	Active
2018	50259-002	Western Uzbekistan Water Supply System Development Project	145,000,000	145,000,000	Active
2017	51240-002	Second Tashkent Province Water Supply Development Project	800,000	800,000	Active
2016	46135-004	Tashkent Province Water Supply Development Project	120,900,000	120,900,000	Active
2015	46135-002	Jizzakh Sanitation System Development Project	81,000,000	81,000,000	Active
2013	45366-004	Solid Waste Management Improvement Project	69,000,000	69,000,000	Active
2011	41340-013	Advanced Electricity Metering Project in Bukhara, Jizzakh, and Samarkand	150,000,000	150,000,000	Active
		Subtotal	949,780,000	949,780,000	
		World Bank			
2020	P162263	Water Services and Institutional Support Program	231,080,000	224,000,000	Active
2019	P168180	Institutional Capacity Building Project	33,000,000	33,000,000	Active
2018	P162929	Medium-Size Cities Integrated Urban Development Project	120,000,000	100,000,000	Active
2018	P146206	District Heating Energy Efficiency Project	140,000,000	140,000,000	Active
2016	P151746	Modernization of Real Property Registration and Cadastre	25,000,000	20,000,000	Active
2016	P156584	Modernization and Upgrade of Transmission Substations	196,000,000	150,000,000	Active
		Subtotal	745,080,000	667,000,000	
		European Bank for Reconstruction and Development			
2020	51856	Tashkent Power Loan	190,600,000	190,600,000	Reviewed
2019	50996	Climate Resilience Water Supply Project	400,000,000	200,000,000	Reviewed

Year	Project ID	Project Title	Project Cost ($)	Commitment ($)	Status
2018	49214	Tashkent District Heating - Tashteploenergo Project	100,000,000	100,000,000	Signed
2018	49277	Tashkent Water Improvement Project	30,000,000	30,000,000	Signed
2018	49213	Tashkent District Heating - Tashteplocentral Project	50,000,000	50,000,000	Signed
		Subtotal	770,600,000	570,600,000	
European Investment Bank					
2019	20180199	Uzbekistan District Heating Loan	226,476,950	108,374,723	Approved
2018	20180198	Uzbekistan Energy Efficiency Loan	108,374,723	108,374,723	Active
2018	20180127	Uzbekistan Water Framework Loan	314,286,697	108,374,723	Active
		Subtotal	649,138,370	325,124,169	
Islamic Development Bank					
2016	N/A	Reconstruction and Expansion of Sewerage Systems of Gulistan, Shirin, and Yangiyer	57,500,000	57,500,000	Active
2013	N/A	Efficient Outdoor Lighting for Tashkent City Project	36,000,000	36,000,000	Active
		Subtotal	93,500,000	93,500,000	
Japan International Cooperation Agency					
2017	UZB-P15	Tashkent Thermal Power Cogeneration Plant Construction Project	107,000,000	107,000,000	Active
Asian Infrastructure Investment Bank					
2020	Special Fund	Karakalpakstan and Khorezm Water Supply and Sanitation Project	4,704,000	4,704,000	Active
Agence Française de Développement					
2016	N/A	Modernization of the Integrated Solid Waste Management in the City of Samarkand	28,966,844	28,966,844	Active
OPEC Fund for International Development					
2019	N/A	Improvement of Water Supply in Yangikurgan District and the City of Namangan Project	71,094,000	53,096,000	Active
		Total	3,419,863,214	2,799,771,013	

Note: This table does not include technical assistance or knowledge products.

References

Agency for Urbanization. *Urbanization Development Concept*. Unpublished.

Akimov, A. and D. Banister. 2011. Urban Transport in Post-Communist Tashkent. *Comparative Economic Studies*. 53. pp. 721–755. http://dx.doi.org/10.1057/ces.2011.18.

Asian Development Bank (ADB). Uzbekistan: Climate Adaptive Water Resources Management in the Aral Sea Basin Sector Project. https://www.adb.org/projects/53120-001/main#project-pds-collapse.

ADB. Uzbekistan: Mortgage Market Sector Development Program. https://www.adb.org/projects/51348-001/main#project-pds.

————. Uzbekistan: Second Tashkent Province Water Supply Development Project Report https://www.adb.org/projects/51240-001/main#project-pds.

————. 2006. *Technical Assistance to the Republic of Uzbekistan for the Transport Sector Strategy (2006–2020)*. Manila. December. https://www.adb.org/sites/default/files/project-document/66621/37691-01-uzb-tacr.pdf.

————. 2014. Enabling GrEEEn Cities: An Operational Framework for Integrated Urban Development in Southeast Asia. *ADB Southeast Asia Working Paper Series* No. 9. Manila. November. https://www.adb.org/sites/default/files/publication/149685/southeast-asia-wp-9.pdf.

————. 2018. *Mortgage Market Development Program—Housing Policy and Subsidy Component*. Consultant's report. Manila (TA 9479-UZB).

————. 2018. *Strategy 2030: Achieving a Prosperous, Inclusive, Resilient and Sustainable Asia and the Pacific*. https://www.adb.org/sites/default/files/institutional-document/435391/strategy-2030-main-document.pdf.

————. 2019. Uzbekistan: Country Partnership Strategy 2019–2023. Manila. May. https://www.adb.org/sites/default/files/institutional-document/510251/cps-uzb-2019-2023.pdf.

————. 2019. *Project Concept Paper: Uzbekistan: Sustainable Solid Waste Management Project*. June. https://www.adb.org/sites/default/files/project-documents/51034/51034-002-cp-en.pdf.

————. 2020. *Technical Assistance to the Republic of Uzbekistan for Preparing Urban Development and Improvement Projects: Strategic Urban and Regional Development Planning for Syrdarya and Djizzak Regions*. Manila.

————. 2021. *Asian Development Outlook: Financing a Green and Inclusive Recovery*. Manila. April. https://www.adb.org/publications/series/asian-development-outlook.

————. 2021. Uzbekistan. *Asian Development Bank Member Fact Sheet*. Manila. April. https://www.adb.org/sites/default/files/publication/27811/uzb-2020.pdf.

Bekzhanova, T. K. and A. B. Temirova. 2019. Non-Observed Economy as a Part of the Developing Economy. *Reports of the National Academy of Sciences of the Republic of Kazakhstan*. 2 (324). pp. 215–222. Tashkent.

Burunciuc, L. et al. 2018. How Uzbekistan is Transforming into an Open Economy. *Brookings*. 20 December. https://www.brookings.edu/blog/future-development/2018/12/20/how-uzbekistan-is-transforming-into-an-open-economy/.

Center for Economic Research. 2009. Urbanization and Industrialization in Uzbekistan: Challenges, Problems and Prospects. *Policy Brief* 2009/01. Tashkent. https://unece.org/fileadmin/DAM/hlm/prgm/cph/experts/uzbekistan/03_land_admin_and_urban_devt/Urbanization_and_industrialization_in_Uzbekistan_challenges__problems_and_prospects.pdf.

Central Asia Regional Economic Cooperation. CAREC Program. https://www.carecinstitute.org/carec-program/.

Central Intelligence Agency (CIS). Central Asia: Uzbekistan. Environment—Current Issues. https://www.cia.gov/library/publications/the-world-factbook/geos/uz.html.

CIS Legislation. About Privatization of the Parcels of Land of Nonagricultural Appointment. https://cis-legislation.com/document.fwx?rgn=117968.

CIS Legislation. Council of Ministers Decree No. 450: Regulations of the Urbanization Agency. https://cis-legislation.com/document.fwx?rgn=116112.

CIS Legislation. Presidential Decree of the Republic of Uzbekistan of August 13, 2019. No. UP-5780. https://cis-legislation.com/document.fwx?rgn=118052.

CIS Legislation. 2019. Presidential Decree of the Republic of Uzbekistan of February 7, 2017. No. UP-4947. https://cis-legislation.com/document.fwx?rgn=94327.

Cities Development Initiative for Asia (CDIA). Project Preparation Study for the ADB Integrated Urban Development Project in Uzbekistan. Inception Report. March 2020). Unpublished.

CDIA. Developing Integrated Solutions for Urban Issues in Uzbekistan. 6 April. https://cdia.asia/2020/04/06/26217/.

Communal Services Agency of the Republic of Uzbekistan. 2017. *Initial Environmental Examination: Western Uzbekistan Water Supply System Development Project* (prepared for ADB). https://www.adb.org/sites/default/files/project-documents/50259/50259-002-iee-en_0.pdf.

Demographia. 2021. *Demographia World Urban Areas*. 17th edition. June. http://www.demographia.com/db-worldua.pdf.

The Economist. 2019. Country of the Year: Which Nation Improved the Most in 2019? London. 21 December. https://www.economist.com/leaders/2019/12/21/which-nation-improved-the-most-in-2019.

Energy Central. 2020. Uzbekistan Adopted the Concept of Supplying the Country with Electric Energy for 2020–2030. 4 May. https://energycentral.com/news/uzbekistan-adopted-concept-supplying-country-electric-energy-2020%E2%80%932030.

Energy Sector Management Assistance Program. 2018. Uzbekistan: Keeping Urban Dwellers Warm. 12 July. https://www.esmap.org/uzbekistan_keeping_urban_dwellers_warm.

Environment Conflict and Cooperation Platform. Rogun Dam Conflict between Tajikistan and Uzbekistan. https://library.ecc-platform.org/conflicts/rogun-dam-tajikistan.

European Investment Bank. 2019. EIB and Uzbekistan Take First Steps Towards a EUR 100M Investment Program for the Recovery of the Aral Sea. 24 September. https://www.eib.org/en/press/all/2019-226-eib-and-uzbekistan-take-first-steps-towards-a-eur-100-m-investment-program-for-the-recovery-of-the-aral-sea.

Frankopan, P. 2018. *The New Silk Roads: The Present and Future of the World*. London.

Global Cement. 2020. State Committee on Ecology and Environmental Protection Suspends Cement Production at SingLida Plant. 26 February. https://www.globalcement.com/news/item/10507-state-committee-on-ecology-and-environmental-protection-suspends-cement-production-at-singlida-plant.

Global Cement. 2020. Uzbekistan Starts Pollution Monitoring. 22 January. https://www.globalcement.com/news/item/10346-uzbekistan-starts-pollution-monitoring.

Global Facility for Disaster Reduction and Recovery. Uzbekistan. https://www.gfdrr.org/en/uzbekistan.

Global Facility for Disaster Reduction and Recovery. Uzbekistan—Urban Flood. http://thinkhazard.org/en/report/261-uzbekistan/UF (accessed 24 June 2020).

Government of Uzbekistan. 1992. *Constitution of the Republic of Uzbekistan*. Chapter 21.

Government of Uzbekistan, Ministry of Economy and Industry. National Development Strategy of the Republic of Uzbekistan until 2030. Unpublished.

Government of Uzbekistan, Ministry of Energy. Concept Note for Ensuring Electricity Supply in Uzbekistan in 2020–2030. http://minenergy.uz/uploads/01261b5c-9c52-2846-9fcf-e252a67917e6_media_.pdf.

Government of Uzbekistan, Ministry of Foreign Affairs. About Aral, Time and Again. https://mfa.uz/en/press/news/2018/12/17146/.

Government of Uzbekistan, Ministry of Foreign Affairs. Protection of the Environment is an Important Factor in Ensuring Public Health. https://mfa.uz/en/press/news/2018/02/13838/.

Government of Uzbekistan, Ministry of Housing and Communal Services. Water Services and Institutional Support Program: Environmental and Social Management Framework. http://documents.worldbank.org/curated/en/573801574931049910/text/Environmental-and-Social-Management-Framework.txt.

Government of Uzbekistan, Ministry of Investment and Foreign Trade. Free Economic Zones. https://mift.uz/en.

Grütter, J. M. and K. J. Kim. 2019. E-Mobility Options for ADB Developing Member Countries. *ADB Sustainable Development Working Paper Series* No. 60. Manila: ADB. https://www.adb.org/sites/default/files/publication/494566/sdwp-060-e-mobility-options-adb-dmcs.pdf.

International Finance Corporation. 2019. Country Private Sector Diagnostics: Creating Markets in Uzbekistan. World Bank Group Presentation to the Government of Uzbekistan. Tashkent. 18 February. https://www.ifc.org/wps/wcm/connect/bac596d6-322f-4e78-9368-bd3bf32c18ae/UZB+CPSD+Launch+Presentation_English.pdf?MOD=AJPERES.

International Monetary Fund. 2019. Article IV Consultation Staff Report. Washington, DC. 9 May. https://www.imf.org/en/Publications/CR/Issues/2019/05/09/Republic-of-Uzbekistan-2019-Article-IV-Consultation-Press-Release-and-Staff-Report-46884.

International Organization for Migration. Uzbekistan. https://www.iom.int/countries/uzbekistan (accessed 01 May 2020).

IQAir. 2020. *World Air Quality Report: Region & City PM2.5 Ranking*. Switzerland. https://www.iqair.com/blog/press-releases/covid-19-reduces-air-pollution-in-most-countries.

Investment Promotion Agency. Fuel Energy Complex. https://invest.gov.uz/investor/tek/.

Izvorski, I. et al. 2019. *Uzbekistan Public Expenditure Review*. Washington, DC: World Bank. http://documents.worldbank.org/curated/en/471601582557360839/pdf/Uzbekistan-Public-Expenditure-Review.pdf.

Japan International Cooperation Agency. 2016. Preparatory Survey (F/S) for Tashkent Thermal Power Cogeneration Plant Construction Project and Master Plan Study in the Republic of Uzbekistan. 26 May. https://openjicareport.jica.go.jp/pdf/12260816.pdf.

Jefferson, M. 1939. The Law of the Primate City. *Geographical Review*. 29 (2). https://doi.org/10.2307/209944.

Kļaviņš, M., A. Azizov, and J. Zaļoksnis. 2014. *Environment, Pollution, Development: The Case of Uzbekistan*. Riga: UL Press.

KUN.UZ. 2019. Uzbekistan Heatwave Temperatures to Reach 42°C. 8 July. https://kun.uz/en/news/2019/07/08/uzbekistan-heatwave-temperatures-to-reach-42c.

Lall, S. and M. Lebrand. 2019. Who Wins, Who Loses? Understanding the Spatially Differentiated Effects of the Belt and Road Initiative. *Policy Research Working Paper 8806*. Washington, DC: World Bank. https://openknowledge.worldbank.org/handle/10986/31535.

Linn, J. F. 2010. Protection Against Severe Earthquake Risks in Central Asia. Brookings. 23 March. https://www.brookings.edu/opinions/protection-against-severe-earthquake-risks-in-central-asia/.

O'zsanoatqurilishmateriallari. On the issues of approval of the main parameters of the program "Obod makhalla" and ensuring their execution. http://uzsm.uz/en/documents/1686/19762/#.

Observatory of Economic Complexity. Uzbekistan. https://oec.world/en/profile/country/uzb/.

Organisation for Economic Co-operation and Development. 2019. Sustainable Infrastructure for Low-Carbon Development in Central Asia and the Caucasus: Hotspot Analysis and Needs Assessment. 19 December. https://www.oecd-ilibrary.org/sites/d1aa6ae9-en/index.html?itemId=/content/publication/d1aa6ae9-en.

Rasanayagam, J. 2011. Informal Economy, Informal State: The Case of Uzbekistan. *International Journal of Sociology and Social Policy*. 31 (11/12). pp. 681–696. Aberdeen. https://abdn.pure.elsevier.com/en/publications/informal-economy-informal-state-the-case-of-uzbekistan.

Seitz, W. 2020. Free Movement and Affordable Housing—Public Preferences for Reform in Uzbekistan. *Policy Research Working Paper* 9107. Washington, DC: World Bank. January.

Shardakova, L. Yu., M. L. Arushanov, and N. R. Rakhmatova. Researches of Atmospheric Air Quality in Uzbekistan. Tashkent: Hydrometeorological Research Institute. http://www.unoosa.org/documents/pdf/psa/activities/2007/graz/presentations/06_07.pdf.

State Committee of the Republic of Uzbekistan for Ecology and Environmental Protection. 2019. *Initial Environmental Examination: Sustainable Solid Waste Management Project in Uzbekistan* (prepared for ADB). https://www.adb.org/sites/default/files/project-documents/51034/51034-002-iee-en.pdf.

Stronski, P. 2010. Tashkent: Forging a Soviet City (1930–1966). Pittsburgh: University of Pittsburgh Press.

Thurman, M. 2011. *Natural Disaster Risks in Central Asia: A Synthesis*. United Nations Development Programme. https://www.geonode-gfdrrlab.org/documents/801.

Transparency International. Corruption Perception Index. 2019. https://www.transparency.org/en/cpi/2019/index/nzl (accessed 01 May 2020).

Transparency International. Country Data. Uzbekistan. https://www.transparency.org/en/countries/uzbekistan# (accessed 01 May 2020).

Tukmadiyeva, M. 2016. *Propiska* as a Tool of Discrimination in Central Asia. *Central Asia Fellowship Papers* No. 12. https://centralasiaprogram.org/archives/9114.

United Nations Conference on Trade and Development. 2019. *World Investment Report 2019: Special Economic Zones*. Geneva. https://unctad.org/en/PublicationsLibrary/wir2019_en.pdf.

United Nations Economic Commission for Europe. 2015. *Country Profiles in Housing and Land Management—Uzbekistan*. Geneva. https://www.unece.org/fileadmin/DAM/hlm/documents/Publications/CP_Uzbekistan_withCorr.EN.pdf.

United Nations Environment Programme. Air Quality Policies. https://wedocs.unep.org/bitstream/handle/20.500.11822/17141/Uzbekistan.pdf?sequence=1&isAllowed=y.

United Nations Framework Convention on Climate Change. Intended Nationally Determined Contributions of the Republic of Uzbekistan (INDC). https://www4.unfccc.int/sites/ndcstaging/PublishedDocuments/Uzbekistan%20First/INDC%20Uzbekistan%2018-04-2017_Eng.pdf.

United Nations Framework Convention on Climate Change. *Uzbekistan: Preparation of the Third National Communication under the UN Framework Convention on Climate Change (UNFCCC).* https://unfccc.int/sites/default/files/resource/TNC%20of%20Uzbekistan%20under%20UNFCCC_english_n.pdf.

University of Central Asia, et al. 2012. *Sustainable Mountain Development in Central Asia. From Rio 1992 to 2012 and Beyond.* http://www.fao.org/fileadmin/user_upload/mountain_partnership/docs/Central-Asia-Mountains.pdf.

Uzbekistan State Commission of Statistics. Demographic Indicators. https://stat.uz/en/open-data/181-ofytsyalnaia-statystyka-en/6383-demography.

Uzbekistan State Commission of Statistics. National Accounts. https://stat.uz/en/181-ofytsyalnaia-statystyka-en/6373-national-accounts.

Uzbekistan State Commission of Statistics. Sample Household Survey. https://stat.uz/en/550-useful-information/7198-sample-household-survey.

Uzbekistan State Commission of Statistics. Total Income of the Population. https://stat.uz/uploads/docs/Aholi_umumiy_daromadlari_eng_24.07.2019.pdf.

Uzbekistan State Commission of Statistics. Volume of Gross Domestic Product of the Republic of Uzbekistan by Types of Economic Activities. http://web.stat.uz/open_data/en/3.3%20Volume_GDP_by_type_activity_eng.pdf.

World Bank. Climate Change Knowledge Portal. Uzbekistan. https://climateknowledgeportal.worldbank.org/country/uzbekistan/vulnerability (accessed 01 May 2020).

World Bank. Key Issues for Consideration on the Proposed Rogun Hydropower Project. http://pubdocs.worldbank.org/en/339251488268367141/World-Bank-Note-Key-Issues-for-Consideration-on-Proposed-Rogun-Hydropower-Project-eng.pdf.

World Bank. Sustaining Market Reforms in Uzbekistan Development Policy Operation. https://projects.worldbank.org/en/projects-operations/project-detail/P168280?lang=en.

World Bank. Uzbekistan Urban Policy Note. Unpublished.

World Bank. 2015. The Case of Uzbekistan: Social Impact Analysis of Water Supply and Sanitation Services in Central Asia. Washington, DC. November. http://documents.worldbank.org/curated/en/860101467994584583/pdf/97832-REVISED-Box394849B-ENGLISH-report-en-ebook.pdf.

World Bank. 2016. Uzbekistan Moves Towards Proactive Approach to Disaster Risk Management. 14 December. https://www.worldbank.org/en/news/feature/2016/12/14/uzbekistan-moves-towards-proactive-approach-to-disaster-risk-management.

World Bank. 2018. District Heating Energy Efficiency Project. Project Appraisal Document. Washington, DC. 3 January. http://documents.worldbank.org/curated/en/591171517108418870/pdf/Uzbekistan-PAD-01052018.pdf.

World Bank. 2018. Uzbekistan: Medium-Size Cities Integrated Urban Development Project. Project Appraisal Document. Washington, DC. 21 November. http://documents.worldbank.org/curated/en/696861545447788756/pdf/UZ-PAD-SECPO-Final-P162929-vF-11292018-636810265761885453.pdf.

World Bank. 2019. *Uzbekistan Country Economic Update: Toward a New Economy*. Washington, DC. https://documents.worldbank.org/en/publication/documents-reports/documentdetail/866501562572675697/uzbekistan-toward-a-new-economy-country-economic-update.

World Bank. 2020. Water Services and Institutional Support Project. Project Appraisal Document. Washington, DC. 20 February. http://documents.worldbank.org/curated/en/802111584324088462/pdf/Uzbekistan-Water-Services-and-Institutional-Support-Project.pdf.

World Health Organization. *Climate Change Adaptation to Protect Human Health*. https://www.who.int/globalchange/projects/adaptation/PHE-adaptation-final-Uzbekistan.pdf?ua=1.

World Population Review. Uzbekistan Population 2020. https://worldpopulationreview.com/countries/uzbekistan-population/ (accessed 1 May 2020).

www.ingramcontent.com/pod-product-compliance
Lightning Source LLC
Chambersburg PA
CBHW050049220326
41599CB00045B/7342